THE *THINKING CLEARLY* SERIES
Series editor: Clive Calver

The *Thinking Clearly* series sets out the main issues in a variety of important subjects. Written from a mainstream Christian standpoint, the series combines clear biblical teaching with up-to-date scholarship. Each of the contributors is an authority in his or her field. The series is written in straightforward everyday language, and each volume includes a range of practical applications and guidance for further reading.

The series has two main aims:
1. To help Christians understand their faith better.
2. To show how Christian truths can illuminate matters of crucial importance in our society.

THE *THINKING CLEARLY* SERIES

Series editor: Clive Calver

The End Times

JOHN E HOSIER

MONARCH
BOOKS

First published by Monarch Books 2000

ISBN 1 85424 500 7

British Library Cataloguing Data
A catalogue record for this book is available
from the British Library.

Designed and produced for the publishers by
Bookprint Creative Services
P.O. Box 827, BN21 3YJ, England
Printed in Great Britain.

Contents

Introduction

Martin Luther is reported to have said that if he knew Christ was returning tomorrow he would plant a tree today. I've tried that statement on several people to find they are usually mystified by it. To me it simply reveals the attitude of a very energetic Christian who, while living with the sure and certain hope of Christ's return, was not going to waste a moment before that great event.

In a way that is what this book is all about. Christians have a confident expectation of the return of Jesus, but there is not a moment to lose before he comes again. The return of Jesus, while certain, also raises some of the most difficult areas to resolve in terms of detail. This book gives an overview of these difficulties and suggests some answers. However the doctrine of eschatology, or the end times is not only about the return of Jesus, it includes a number of other issues as well. There is the matter of our own personal end time, judgement, the nature of heaven and hell, and even how we are to regard the nation of Israel now and at the end of history.

But when we consider all these issues does it make any real difference to us now? My answer would be that our eschatology directly affects our ecclesiology, or what we believe about the end times will affect the way we are building the local church. So eschatology is very important. Christians want to know what is going to happen to them when they die, and the Church always needs help to clarify her present mission. This book attempts to take a serious look at these matters.

These chapters are loosely based on material I have been lecturing, teaching and preaching for a number of years. There have been many influences on my thinking, via books and other teachers. Some of them I mention by name in the following chapters. Most of them I cannot now probably name, although I am grateful to them all.

I am particularly grateful for the practical help of two secretaries, Sharon and Emma. And I would like to thank my wife for her endless patience in sitting through numerous lectures on the Tribulation, the Millennium and other End Time subjects.

1

A Common Agreement

As we will be looking at a subject which is acknowledged by everyone to be quite complex it will be helpful to start with something simple! We can define some basic terms and look at areas where there is general agreement among all evangelical Christians. We know Jesus is going to return even if we are confused about the details and order of events.

A Common Agreement

All of us think about the end of the world. For some it can be kind of idle speculation, for others a matter about which they really worry. Probably most of us have known times when we have felt it could happen imminently.

I retain a strong memory of the Cuban missile crisis in 1962. I was training to be a Navigating Officer with BP Oil Tankers and at home on leave during the crisis itself. The company required me to attend a lecture in central London, though for what purpose I cannot now imagine as it included a film of missiles being launched and destroyed. Sitting through the action was very unnerving, for my mind kept straying to the current crisis between Russia and America and to the thought that, even as I watched a film about missiles, the United States might be intercepting ships carrying nuclear weapons to Cuba. If that happened there was a real possibility that a third World War would begin and we would all be history.

Men and women have always been fascinated about the end times and the end of the world. Many have tried to fix dates for the final cataclysm and, at times in history such as the Cuban missile crisis, have wondered if the end was now at hand.

Christians are the only people who really know how the world will end, although they disagree among themselves as to the details of the programme!

The Christian doctrine concerning the end times is known as eschatology, taken from the Greek word 'eschatos' meaning last things. The Bible has plenty to say about the last things – indeed that may cause something of a problem. There is so much teaching on this subject in the Bible that we are faced with the challenge of sorting it all out. Sometimes we are confused! Sometimes we are very definite in our opinions, only to find that other Christians are equally definite in their rather different opinions.

27 per cent of the Bible is made up of prediction about the future. It is calculated that the return of Christ is fore-told 319 times and almost every book in the New Testament refers to it.

It appears that the return of Christ was first prophesied right back in the beginning of human history, before the Flood. We read in the book of Jude: 'Enoch, the seventh from Adam, prophesied about these men: "see, the Lord is coming with thousands upon thousands of his holy ones to judge everyone, and to convict all the ungodly of all the ungodly acts they have done in an ungodly way, and of all the harsh words ungodly sinners have spoken against him"' (Jude 14,15). So the earliest reference to the return of Jesus Christ is found in the last but one book of the Bible!

The final mention of the return of Christ is at the end of the last book of the Bible: 'He who testifies to these things says, "Yes, I am coming soon." Amen. Come, Lord Jesus' (Rev 22:20).

With so much biblical material to look at, we often need to decide whether a particular scripture is to be understood literally or metaphorically. Sometimes a text is very clearly picture language or metaphor. Jesus talks about the separation of sheep and goats on the day of judgement (Matt 25:31–33), but I know of no one who believes that heaven will literally be populated with sheep and hell with goats! Sometimes, however, the matter is not nearly so clear. What about the 1,000 years of Revelation chapter 20 – is this a literal time span or is it symbolic of a long period of time? Then there are the Old Testament prophecies of a wonderful, prosperous and peaceful age. We read the promise, 'They will beat their swords into ploughshares and their spears into pruning hooks. Nation will not take up sword against nation, nor will they train for war anymore' (Isa 2.4). Will this literally happen on earth, or are we to see this as prophecy which will have a spiritual fulfilment in the Church? Could the reference mean not that there will be universal peace on earth, but that the Church of God will enjoy peace? Many times there is a debate over these and other prophecies. Evangelical Christians will always seek to take scripture as literally as possible unless there is a clear reason not to do so.

There are three words used in the New Testament for the return of Christ that are worth taking note of:

1. *Parousia*. This Greek word has been carried over directly into the English language. It refers to an arrival and was used of the arrival of a royal visitor. If the Queen was about to make an official visit to our town or city we could speak of her Parousia. 'Concerning the coming of

the Lord Jesus Christ . . .', (1 Thess 2:1). The word 'coming' here is the word *parousia*.

2. *Epiphaneia*. This word means 'an appearance'. It was used of the appearance of a god to his worshippers in Greek mythology. It would be used for a sovereign who would appear to receive the acclamation of the people – just as when the Queen appears on the balcony of Buckingham Palace on some great state occasion. 'And the lawless one will be revealed, whom the Lord Jesus will overthrow with the breath of his mouth and destroy by the splendour of his coming' (2 Thess 2:8). Here the word for 'coming' is *epiphaneia* and not *parousia*. So the reference is to the splendour of Christ's appearance when he comes.

3. *Apokalupsis*. This word means 'uncover' in the sense of unveiling or revealing glory – as when a sovereign would appear in crown and robes. There is definitely a sense of the Queen's majesty being revealed when she wears a state crown and royal robes for, say, the State Opening of Parliament. '. . . This will happen when the Lord Jesus is revealed from heaven in blazing fire and with his powerful angels' (2 Thess 1:7). The word 'revealed' here is *apokalupsis*.

If we put these three words together we learn that Christ will come again, his appearance will draw the acclamation of the peoples of the world, and his glory and majesty will be revealed. The Scripture gives us a picture of this in the Book of Acts. Angels appear to the disciples as they gaze into the sky following the Ascension and disappearance of Christ from their view. The angels assure them that Jesus will return in the same manner as they have seen him go. He ascended from the Mount of Olives in a cloud, with angels present and the disciples looking on. So he will appear again, to stand, many believe, on the Mount of Olives once more. He will come with the clouds. That recalls the Old Testament images of the Shekinah glory of God. He will come with the angels, who will gather in the elect from the ends of the earth. He will be seen as he appears by his disciples (and indeed by all other peoples of the world). Jesus will return in the same way that he left.

Common beliefs

All evangelical Christians are committed to a belief in the Parousia, or coming again of Jesus. Differences arise when they begin to discuss the exact order of events. But there are a number of basic truths that are common to all who believe in Christ's return. It is worth mentioning these before we venture into more controversial areas.

1. Christ's coming again is certain in that it is confirmed from every section of Scripture. In the Old Testament it is seen in the prophecy of Zechariah, 'Then the Lord my God will come, and all the holy ones with him' (Zech 14:5). The Gospels, the Acts, the letters of Paul, and the Book of Revelation speak repeatedly of Christ's return. In fact there are over 300 references to this event in the New Testament. It is not surprising therefore that the return of Christ was the eager expectation of the early Church.
2. Then again, the *way* in which Christ will return is commonly agreed. It will be a personal return, for Paul

says to the Thessalonians that Christ himself will return. It will certainly be a glorious return, and will be visible for all to see. 'Look, he is coming with the clouds, and every eye will see him . . .' (Rev 1:7). We may speculate on how everyone will see the return of Christ when we live on a round planet. How will Australians see him as well as those in England? Some have suggested that it will be a televised event! One can imagine that it would attract maximum viewing figures. But everything to do with Christ's return will be supernatural and it would seem unwise to over-speculate in certain areas of detail.

When Christ came the first time, he was born in humble circumstances; very few were aware of his birth. He was probably a carpenter for most of his life and was ordinary to look at, for the prophet Isaiah said he had no beauty that we should desire him. He was mocked, spat upon and nailed to a Roman gibbet. But when he returns, even the stars and planets will fall. Everyone will see him; he will be recognised as the Lord of all. His appearance will be dazzling and while his followers acclaim him, his persecutors will weep.

3. There is definitely clear *purpose* in Christ's return. He is not coming again merely because he said so but he will achieve certain definite aims. He will wind up history and bring in eternity. The following will be affected:

   • The Church will be married to Christ. 'Let us rejoice and be glad and give him glory! For the wedding of the Lamb has come, and his bride has made herself ready' (Rev 19:7).
   • All mankind will be judged. 'And I saw the dead, great and small, standing before the throne, and

books were opened . . . The dead were judged according to what they had done as recorded in the books' (Rev 20:12).

- All creation will be transformed. 'But in keeping with his promise we are looking forward to a new heaven and a new earth, the home of righteousness' (2 Peter 3:13).

We will look at these results of Christ's return later in this book. We simply note here that nothing and nobody will be unaffected by the return of Jesus.

4. The time of Christ's return is unknown. This hasn't stopped unwise people trying to work it out! It isn't just Jehovah's Witnesses who have fixed particular dates for Christ's return. There are frequent examples of sincere Christian believers who make their own suggestions. The books of Daniel and Revelation contain many references to a certain number of days or weeks. This gives opportunity for the enterprising believer to devise mathematical schemes to determine the date of Christ's return. In recent years I have read confident predictions of the Rapture taking place on 14th May 1997 and the Return of Christ on 14th May 2004. However the Bible tells us that even Christ's own knowledge of the time of his return was limited and so we cannot possibly know (Mark 13:32). The only thing we can say with absolute confidence is that his return is closer than it used to be.

These are agreed truths about Christ's return among evangelical Christians. In the following chapters we will be looking at differences of opinion about details and the order of events. None of these differences obscure the fact that Christ will certainly return.

We can recall that all the Old Testament prophecies about Christ's first coming were fulfilled in detail. In the New Testament we have even more descriptions and more numerous prophecies concerning his Second Coming.

Christ will come again.

2

The Big Trouble

Jesus warned his disciples of trouble to come and that there are certain clear signs that precede his return. Many Christians have been fascinated about the identity of the Antichrist. There has been enough wrong speculation about this over the centuries to warn us of the dangers of trying to come up with a name. Also many have treated the mark of the Beast, the number 666, almost like a game that if we play it right will give us the name of the Antichrist. The number probably does relate to the Greek game of Gematria, but again we would probably be wise not to try and play it.

The Big Trouble

The Bible indicates that we are heading towards big trouble. This is usually referred to as the Tribulation. A much debated issue is whether Christians will have to go through this time of intense trial and suffering which may last for seven years. The figure of seven years comes from Daniel 9:24–27, though many would argue it represents a short period of time. We read of the Tribulation in several places in the New Testament. It appears in the gospels in the parallel chapters of Matthew 24, Mark 13 and Luke 21. But there is also reference to it in Paul's letters and in the book of Revelation.

We face a puzzle with the gospel chapters. In these passages there is an interweaving of details concerning the destruction of Jerusalem and the end of the age. From our perspective these are two very obviously distinct events, distant from one another by at least 1900 years. So we may wonder how two such separate events can be interwoven. From the perspective of the disciples and the Jews, the destruction of Jerusalem and the Temple would have seemed like an end-time event. When it occurred it was certainly the end of their world, as the Jews had known it. Also it is possible to see the destruction of Jerusalem as a pattern of a greater trouble and destruction yet to come. Certainly the time of Jerusalem's destruction in 70 AD was a time of great tribulation. Referring to Herod's Temple in Jerusalem, Jesus said, 'Do you see all these things?' . . . 'I tell you the truth, not one stone here will be left on another; every one will be thrown down' (Matt 24:2).

Let's look at Matthew chapter 24 in more detail. Here Jesus begins to discuss the Temple buildings with his disciples. Although Herod's Temple was still unfinished in the time of Jesus it was already a magnificent construction. Stones used in the building of the Temple weighed up to 100 tons, all moved into place by manual labour. There were columns 47 ft high, their circumferences wide enough for three men to stretch their arms out around the base. Yet Jesus says not one stone will be left on another! This was fulfilled when the Roman soldiers set fire to the Temple and the melted gold filled the seams between the stones causing the soldiers to literally pull the Temple apart.

Signs of Christ's return

Such a predicted event sounds like the end of the world to the disciples, who then ask Jesus when it will happen. Jesus doesn't want his disciples to be deceived, so he gives them four groups of signs concerning his return.

Disasters

There is mention of wars, earthquakes and famines (vv. 6–8). Certainly when these events occur it can seem like the end of the world. Jesus says that these disasters are not to be understood like that. In fact these things have occurred right through human history and will continue to the end. However if you are caught up in them, it's easy enough to believe this might be the end of the world!

Certainly we are aware of earthquakes that have killed thousands, terrible famines – especially in Africa – and many dreadful wars even since the Second World War. But all these disasters warn us of a coming great disaster. These are the beginning of the end, and not the end itself.

However, a time of disaster and crisis is an environment in which a false Christ can arise who will give false hope and make false claims.

The people of God

Universal persecution will take place. God's people will suffer and die right around the world. As a result, the love of many will grow cold and yet the Church will reach the whole world with the gospel (v. 14). It is simply a historical fact that persecution has caused nominal Christians to fall away, but many non-believers come to faith as they observe the witness and courage of persecuted believers. The blood of the martyrs has always been seed for the Church. During the time of such persecution false prophets will arise. Christians are unlikely to be led astray by a false Christ but they are always vulnerable to false prophets.

Jerusalem

We have already noted that there are those who suggest that in Matthew 24 (and parallel chapters) Jesus interweaves the destruction of Jerusalem with prophecies of end-time events. However, it is possible to interpret this scripture as indicating that Jerusalem will also be significantly involved in the events of the very end times and during the Great Tribulation.

We need to particularly note the quotation that Jesus makes from the Book of Daniel in verse 15, 'So when you see standing in the holy place the abomination that causes desolation, spoken of through the prophet Daniel – let the reader understand'. Clearly there is something particular to get hold of here. In 170 BC the Greek tyrant Antiochus Epiphanes desecrated the Jewish Temple by sacrificing a pig on the altar and turning the building into a brothel. Not surprisingly the Jews referred to this as the Abomination of Desolation and there were great celebrations when the Jews, led by Judas Maccabaeus, were victorious over the Syrian-Greek coalition and were able to cleanse the Temple.

With the destruction of the city in 70 AD, the approaching Roman armies, their standards decorated with the image of Caesar (who was worshipped as a god), would once more represent the abomination of desolation. There is, however, the possibility that the final abomination of desolation should be regarded as the Antichrist who will come at the end of the age.

In Mark 13:14 the abomination of desolation actually reads as a 'he' standing where he does not belong. This is a very unusual expression, but could refer to the world ruler who will arise near the end of history at the time of the Great Tribulation. We could then understand that Jesus is making a reference to a man who will set himself up as god in Jerusalem, though whether to take Jerusalem literally as the city or as symbolic of the Church is certainly debated.

As a result of this abomination, worldwide trouble will arise which, unless God kept the time short, would threaten even the elect. Many people will be deceived at that time. Signs, wonders and miracles will be performed, but their origin will be evil and so Christians will need to be aware of the danger. Rumours of Christ having appeared will circulate; Christians are being warned ahead of time so as not to be deceived.

Cosmic

Finally, signs will occur even in the heavenly bodies. Everything in the universe will be shaken. It is at this point that Christians can really look up, for the Son of Man is about to appear in great power and glory.

The Antichrist

We only find the term Antichrist in the letters of John and many today would emphasise the fact that Antichrist is both a principle and a person of evil: '. . . but every spirit that does not acknowledge Jesus is not from God. This is the spirit of the antichrist, which you have heard is coming and even now is already in the world' (1 John 4:3). So the characteristic of this spirit or principle is that of denial. However we also read, 'Dear children, this is the last hour; and as you have heard that the antichrist is coming, even now many antichrists have come . . .' (1 John 2:18). This not only states that there is a spirit of anti-christ, but that we can expect the Antichrist to come at some unspecified time.

We also see a reference to the Antichrist, here called the Man of Lawlessness, in Paul's writings. 'He (the man of lawlessness) will oppose and will exalt himself over every-thing that is called God or is worshipped, so that he sets himself up in God's temple, proclaiming himself to be

God' (2 Thess 2:4). So Paul teaches that in the future Satan will make a last great effort to bring evil to a head in the manifestation of a man of evil. However he will finally be defeated at the appearance of Christ (2 Thess 2:8).

Again in the Book of Revelation we have teaching on the Antichrist, though here called the Beast. Chapter 13 contains much of this material, where we read he will set himself up to be worshipped and also as a world ruler. His power will be both political and ecclesiastical. The Beast will receive his worship from those who are not true Christians and therefore followers of the true Christ. They will receive the number 666, which is the mark of the Beast. A false prophet who will encourage worship of the Beast will support him and will himself be a master of magic and a great deceiver. We remember that Christ warned of such things as he foretold the end of the age.

Finally the false prophet and the Beast are thrown into the lake of fire at the return of Christ (Rev 19:20). The victory of Christ over all evil is certain.

What the Bible would cause us to expect therefore is a spirit of antichrist always at work in the world. We have seen this spirit particularly in atheistic communist regimes. However towards the end of the age there is a final concentration of wickedness in one man, the Antichrist, the Man of Lawlessness or the Beast. But both in 2 Thessalonians and Revelation we are assured of his utter defeat at the coming of Christ.

666

The number 666, which is the mark of the Beast, has long fascinated Christians. Does this number give any clue to his identity? John Stott gives a provocative overview of the history of the Antichrist's identification.

In the post-apostolic centuries of the church Christians have practised considerable ingenuity in trying to identify one of their contemporaries as the man of lawlessness. After the demise of the persecuting emperors and the conversion of Constantine, the Roman emperor no longer seemed a suitable candidate. At first one or other of the Vandal leaders, who raided Roman provinces and finally sacked Rome (455 AD), looked anti-Christian enough to be Antichrist. In the Middle Ages, especially at the time of the Crusades, the Western church identified the man of lawlessness as Muhammad, because he had 'stolen' the Christian holy places and caused many eastern Christians to commit 'apostasy'. Towards the end of the Middle Ages some of the Franciscans saw in the corrupt popes and their proud pretensions an expression of the one who would 'exalt himself' and 'set himself up in God's sanctuary', while at the beginning of the thirteenth century Emperor Frederick II and Pope Gregory IX found satisfaction in calling each other the Antichrist. The early Reformers (Wycliffe in England, the Waldensians in Italy and John Hus in Bohemia) all referred the prophecy to the Pope, or rather to particular popes on account of their corruption, whereas – with greater exegetical insight – the sixteenth-century Reformers, including Luther, Calvin and Zwingli on the Continent, Knox in Scotland and Cranmer in England, believed that the papacy itself was Antichrist. The Roman Catholic leaders of the Counter-Reformation then returned the compliment by identifying Luther as 'the man of sin'. The identification of the Pope as Antichrist continued at least into the seventeenth century. The Westminster Confession (1646), for example, affirms that the Lord Jesus Christ is the head of the church, and not the Pope, who is rather 'that man of sin, and son of perdition, that exalteth himself, in the Church, against Christ and all that is called God'.

During the last two centuries political rather than religious leaders have been put forward as possible Antichrists. Candidates have included Napoleon Bonaparte (because of his arrogant absolutism), Napoleon III, Kaiser Wilhelm, Hitler, Mussolini and Stalin, and certainly strong elements of both godlessness and lawlessness have been seen in these men.[1]

Personally, I lean towards the view that the number of the Beast, 666, is best understood in connection with the Greek game Gematria. In the Greek language letters of the alphabet also carry a numerical value. The game of Gematria involved trying to work out the name behind a given number. In the excavated city of Pompeii there is an inscription 'I love her whose number is 545'! Add up the numerical value of the letters of the name Jesus and they come to 888, a clear contrast to the number of the devil's christ, which is 666. Some have suggested that the numerical value of the Roman Emperor Nero equals 666, but this is incorrect. It is true that the numerical value of the Hebrew letters for Caesar Nero comes to 666, but this seems a bit desperate! It is surely best to see here that the number 666 is obviously a contrast to 888 as the numerical value of the name of Jesus, but much as we try to play the game we will not be able to work out a name for 666. So far many have played the game and suggested a name behind the number 666, but all have been proved wrong!

One ingenious suggestion was that if A = 100, B = 101, etc. then the name Hitler adds up to 666. But why should A = 100? It's certainly another misguided attempt to play the game, though no one could deny that the spirit of antichrist must certainly have been present in Hitler.

One thing is certain, though; whatever the true identity of the Antichrist, in the course of time he will be revealed but also finally destroyed by the splendour of Christ's coming (2 Thess 2:8).

It is often believed that the Antichrist is so-called because he is anti – or against – Christ. This is obviously true, but the Greek preposition 'anti' actually means 'instead of'. So the Antichrist is an 'instead of Christ'. This gives us a clue as to how the Antichrist may be able to establish his position at all. It is possible to speculate that in an increasingly chaotic world scene, with law and order breaking down and perhaps economic collapse, men and women will begin to long for a strong man to take control and sort out the mess. This was surely how Hitler came to power in Germany before the Second World War. He was seen to be a strong leader who would give the German nation confidence and order once again.

The Antichrist might at first look like the answer to the needs of the nations; he may appear to be the strong man or saviour the world needs. His rule therefore will not be one of anarchy but of totalitarianism and absolute control. Established in such a strong position he will then brook no opposition or disloyalty. It is for this reason that Christians will suffer, for their loyalty is to the true Christ and they will not give their worship to another. Even as Daniel's friends would not worship the golden image of Nebuchadnezzar or the early Christians would not declare that 'Caesar is Lord', so Christians in the end times will not bow to the greatest dictator of all and worship the Antichrist. Persecution will be intense, martyrs will be many, but the time will be short. Christ is soon to come again.

Notes

1. John Stott, *The Message of Thessalonians*, (Bible Speaks Today series), IVP, 1991, pp. 165–6.

3

Disappearing Saints

'The Rapture' refers to the time when the believers will be caught away from the earth to meet the Lord in the air. Some have suggested that this event will take place before the Tribulation and therefore the Church will escape the rule of the Antichrist. Others have taught that the more spiritual part of the Church will be raptured half way through the Tribulation leaving the rest to be refined during a period of suffering. The long-term, classical view has been that the Church will be on earth during the whole Tribulation period during which time there will be both successful evangelism and much suffering.

Disappearing Saints

One of the most dramatic events associated with Christ's return is when the Church will be caught up or snatched away from the earth to meet Jesus in the air. This is referred to as 'the Rapture'. The clearest description of it comes in 1 Thessalonians 4:16–17:

> For the Lord himself will come down from heaven, with a loud command, with the voice of the archangel and with the trumpet call of God, and the dead in Christ will rise first. After that, we who are still alive and are left will be caught up together with them in the clouds to meet the Lord in the air. And so we will be with the Lord forever.

That the Church will be snatched away, or raptured, is not in dispute, but there are different viewpoints as to when this will happen. Some Christians speak of Pre-Tribulation Rapture, meaning that the Rapture occurs before the Tribulation, others of Post-Tribulation Rapture, with the Church being snatched away after the

Tribulation is over. There are even some who teach a Mid-Tribulation Rapture, where the Church disappears half way through the Tribulation.

Those who speak of the Church being raptured before the Tribulation must naturally agree to the coming of Christ being in two phases. First he appears in the sky secretly and the Church is snatched away to join him. This is followed by the period of the Tribulation after which Jesus returns openly and visibly for all to see, accompanied by his Church. This later phase of Christ's second coming is normally referred to as the Revelation. What is valuable in this teaching is that it keeps alive the hope of Christ's imminent return. Nothing that has been prophesied needs still to be fulfilled before the Rapture. Christ could come at any moment, even while you are reading this page! Certainly people have been converted under preaching that declares, 'Jesus could return tonight; would you be ready for him?'

Some history

It seems that this particular viewpoint was not taught before about 1830, when a number of streams converged to give impetus to this idea. It was prophesied in a meeting of Edward Irving's church. Edward Irving was a preacher of extraordinary gifting, but lived on the edge of some non-orthodox ideas. His church experienced an outbreak of spiritual gifts that were somewhat uncontrolled. About the same time J. N. Darby, the founder of the Brethren movement, was also giving similar teaching on the Second Coming. But what caused it to become very well-known was its inclusion in the notes of the so-called Scofield Bible, an edition of the King James Version widely read and popular well into the middle part of the 20th century. It is perhaps as well to remind ourselves that notes included in any edition of any translation of the Bible must never be considered as authoritative as the actual biblical text.

Any Moment

While this teaching does keep alive the hope of Christ's return at any moment, it is also prone to a degree of sensationalism. I have read and heard descriptions of a Pre-Tribulation Rapture that place a great emphasis on separation. So there will be separation of believers from unbelievers and therefore of husbands from wives and brothers from sisters as well as neighbours from neighbours and friends from friends.

This is sometimes extended to possible scenarios by some fairly imaginative thinking. So you might walk into the kitchen where your wife has been preparing dinner to find she has suddenly disappeared. Or you might phone your husband at the office to discover suddenly he had vanished from behind his desk. You might be in the park with your children, you turn round for a moment and then looking again you find they have all disappeared. There is even the possibility of some potentially disastrous situations. You could be doing 70 miles an hour along the M25 and in a moment notice various cars out of control and without drivers right in front of you. You could be flying over the Atlantic and discover to your horror that the cockpit crew has suddenly disappeared. There could even be a very nasty shock for a Church attender who discovers in the middle of the preacher's sermon one Sunday morning that suddenly only he and the preacher are left in the Church building!

These kinds of descriptions are the logical outcome of

a belief in a Pre-Tribulation Rapture, but frankly they tend to be almost amusing and entertaining.

The Church in Tribulation

Throughout Christian history the consistent view of the Church has been that she will not escape the Tribulation, but will suffer during it and then be snatched away to meet Christ in the air when he returns at the end of Antichrist's rule. This viewpoint is certainly criticised by those who hold to the more modern teaching of a Pre-Tribulation Rapture.

One major criticism would be that the Second Coming would not contain that element of surprise spoken of in the New Testament (see Matt 24:42–44) if it was known that Christ would return at the end of the Tribulation. However, the New Testament does seem to teach clearly that not everyone will be surprised. Referring to his own return Jesus says to his disciples, 'You will know that it is near' (Mark 13:29).

The Apostle Paul makes the same point:

Now brothers, about times and dates we do not need to write to you, for you know very well that the day of the Lord will come like a thief in the night. While people are saying, 'Peace and safety', destruction will come on them suddenly, as labour pains on a pregnant woman, and they will not escape. But you brothers are not in darkness so that this day should surprise you like a thief. You are all sons of the light and sons of the day. We do not belong to the night or to the darkness. (2 Thess 5:1–5)

So while Jesus will return like a thief in the night – which will catch unbelievers by surprise and therefore be a shock for them – believers will be expecting his return. They will not be in the dark about these things; they have been watching the signs – although they will not of course know the day or the hour of Christ's return.

Those believing in a Pre-Tribulation Rapture will refer to the scriptures that talk of those that are taken and those who are left behind (see Luke 17:34–35). This does not require us to believe that those left behind then remain on earth for the Tribulation, only that at his return believers will be caught up into the air to meet Jesus while unbelievers will be left out of that event and left behind.

It has often been claimed that the imminent return of Jesus Christ was the expectation of the early Church, so how does this square with a Post-Tribulation Rapture? Well again we need to note the full story in the Bible. There are several references that indicate some clear delay before Jesus would return. In 2 Thessalonians chapter 2 Paul quite specifically says that there were those suggesting that he himself was teaching that the Day of the Lord had already come. He argues that in fact the day cannot come until the Man of Lawlessness had appeared, something which clearly had not happened yet.

Moreover, Jesus told Peter that he would be crucified in old age and that John would survive him; so a future time span was to be expected. Again, Jesus said that the gospel of the kingdom would be preached to all nations, and then the end would come. Such a mission is bound to take some length of time.

Other less important arguments are made against a Post-Tribulation Rapture, but overall there seems to be no real reason to question the classical long-term view of the Church that Christ will not return for his people until the Tribulation has ended. Rather than escape the

Tribulation, Christians will suffer in it and there will be many martyrs. Yet whatever the Church's sufferings in the Tribulation, we have the assurance that the time will be short and we can know that we are into the final count-down before the Lord's return.

I have sometimes been asked what I feel about the suggestion that I might be wrong and that Christ may return before the Tribulation. In the final analysis, while Christians may have to agree to differ about this subject, on this one I'd prefer to prepare believers for the Tribulation and then be proved wrong than not prepare them and then discover I was wrong!

In order to deal fairly with the biblical material I do need to mention an apparent contradiction in Mark 13. Jesus says in verse 29 with reference to his return, 'Even so, when you see these things happening, you know that it is near, right at the door.' However he goes on in verses 32 and 33 to say, 'No one knows about that day or hour, not even the angels in heaven, nor the Son, but only the Father. Be on guard! Be alert! You do not know when that time will come.'

So do we know, or don't we? Well, we could argue that we don't know well in advance, but eventually the signs will be in place that will indicate his near return. When my younger son, David, was dating his girlfriend Emma, it was obvious to my wife and myself that the relationship was steadily becoming more serious and more committed. It was also becoming quite a long courtship. Surely, we kept thinking, they are going to announce their engage-ment soon. Late one afternoon David rang me up. 'Guess where I am Dad,' he said. Knowing that he worked in London I made the rather uninspired reply, 'London, I suppose.' 'Well you're wrong,' he said, 'I'm in Paris and the young lady beside me has a diamond ring on her left hand.' I was completely caught out by surprise over an event which, from all the signs I'd read, was definitely going to happen.

On two occasions in my marriage all the signs were present that my wife was going to give birth. Somehow though it didn't remove the surprise of the actual event and indeed on the second occasion we only just made it in time to the hospital! When Jesus comes again we may have read the signs, but it could still be an unexpected moment.

Mid-Tribulation

The view concerning a Mid-Tribulation Rapture, which was taught by Watchman Nee among others, often suggests that only the more faithful part of the Church will be raptured half way through the Tribulation (before the more severe second half) which will leave the less faithful part of the Church to be refined by persecution before the end. This compromise position allows you to leave Christians in the Tribulation *and* get them out! However it is undermined by the fact that there is no section of Scripture that naturally reads to give any real support to this view. Indeed 1 Thessalonians chapter 4, which is the clearest passage on the subject, would indicate that the whole Church is raptured, not just the 'best bit'.

Lance Lambert writes:

However, it is good to remember that aggressive dogmatism on detail in such a complex subject as the second advent is rarely healthy. When it is made an excuse for division or faction, it has become an evil. There are major truths in God's word on which God's people are entitled to be, and indeed should be, dogmatic. There are also areas of detail relating to major truths which are not sufficiently clear to allow such dogmatism. On those details it is good to hold honest convictions, while at the same time remaining open-minded, and maintaining fellowship with those who see them differently. At the risk of repeating myself, one fact needs to be underlined. The Lord Jesus could have made this matter absolutely clear by one short discourse in which he outlined the sequence of events. That this was not so was by design. Instead of giving us a clear-cut and catalogued programme, he calls on us to be ready for him whenever he appears.[1]

Well, I suppose we might respond by saying that Jesus could have foreseen every theological dispute in history and sorted it out in advance. After all, Christians are still divided over water baptism. What is helpful in the above statement is the reminder that, although we may be certain, dogmatic even, in what we believe, we must not become bigoted and divisive in areas of doctrine that are not directly relevant to salvation.

I would also want to add that God has given us minds to search out the truth, and even in these difficult areas it is possible, having studied all the scriptures and listened to the different viewpoints, to come to a confident conclusion.

Obviously I could be wrong, but if I'm still alive when Jesus returns I believe I will have been supported by your fellowship during the Tribulation!

Notes

1.   Lance Lambert, *Till the Day Dawns*, Kingsway, 1982.

4

A Thousand Years

Among Christians the word 'Millennium' refers to the thousand-year reign of Christ. However, the nature of that reign is in dispute. Does Christ reign from heaven throughout the Church Age with the 1000 years being understood as a symbol of that time? Or will Christ reign in some future golden age for the Church when she will see immense success in her evangelism, with most people coming to Christ? Or are we to believe that Christ will literally reign on this planet for 1000 years together with his Church? We have to deal with some rather fancy theological terms here, but none of this should obscure the truth that Jesus is going to return and lead the Church into the eternal age.

A Thousand Years

In the Book of Revelation, chapter 20 and verse 4, we read, 'They came to life and reigned with Christ a thousand years.'

Those few words are at the core of a debate that leads to very different views concerning the return of Jesus. What will happen immediately after Jesus returns? Will we be straight into the eternal age, or is there going to be a further 1000 years of world history when Jesus is again on the earth?

The three best-known opinions on this subject are referred to as Pre-Millennialism, Post-Millennialism and A-Millennialism. The word 'Millennium' is taken from the Latin word for a thousand, and is used of the 1000 years mentioned in Revelation chapter 20.

There are variations even within the three main viewpoints, but let's not over-complicate the already complicated!

Pre-Millennialism

This viewpoint has two distinct expressions known as Historic Pre-Millennialism and Dispensational Pre-Millennialism.

Historic Pre-Millennialism states that Christ will reign on the earth with his Church for 1000 years. Most, but not all, Pre-Millennialists will say that the Church passes through the Tribulation and does not escape it.

What will happen during this 1000 years? Reference is made to the Old Testament prophecies that so far seem to remain unfulfilled. These speak of a time of peace and prosperity upon the earth. So, the reaper will be overtaken by the ploughman and the planter by the one treading grapes (Amos). Swords will be beaten into ploughshares; spears into pruning hooks and nation will not take up sword against nation nor train for war anymore (Micah). The cow will feed with the bear, the lion will eat straw like the ox, the infant will play near the hole of the cobra and the young child put his hand into the viper's nest (Isaiah).

In short, the 1000-year reign of Christ on the earth will be a golden age. It will be safe, secure, peaceful and prosperous. All the peoples of the earth will enjoy the benefits of such a government; the Sermon on the Mount will become a reality.

Pre-Millennialists will claim that theirs is the clearest, most straightforward interpretation of Revelation chapter 20 and therefore the right interpretation. It also means that the presently unfulfilled prophecies of the Old Testament can have a definite, literal fulfilment.

However there are many objections made to this. Revelation chapter 20 is the only place in the Bible where the 1000 years is mentioned at all. Is it right to take an obscure passage from a difficult book in the Bible and then try and support it from Old Testament prophecies which could be understood in a totally different way?

Also the objection is made that Revelation chapter 20 does not say that Christ reigns *on the earth*; simply that Christ reigns for 1000 years. Revelation is surely giving us an insight into the heavenly realities behind the visible world scene. Things may look bad on earth and Christians may be martyred, but those who may appear to have lost so much will have lost nothing for Christ reigns all the time. The 1000 years then symbolises the whole length of the Church age. We need a symbolic number because we don't know the time of Christ's return.

Pre-Millennialism also requires us to believe that a glorified Christ will reign with his glorified saints on earth alongside sinful, unglorified, humanity. Many claim that this stretches our credibility beyond reasonable limits. Moreover, if some of the unconverted are saved during this millennium, and here there seem to be different opinions, then clearly not all are converted because Satan is able to stir up a final rebellion at the end of the 1000 years and he obviously has people he can call on. How could many not be converted when they see Christ and the Church on the earth?

There are many other objections, but these are among the most telling.

The great advantage of this viewpoint is that it seeks to take all Scripture as literally as possible, including Revelation chapter 20, and it looks forward to a time when all the peoples of the earth will be able to see and enjoy the direct government of Jesus Christ. What a wonderful world that will be!

Dispensational Pre-Millennialism sees all of history

divided into (usually) seven dispensations, and it has a distinctly Jewish flavour. Presently we are in the dispensation of grace, the Church Age. This will be followed by the dispensation of the Kingdom, the Millennium, during which the nation of Israel will come into the full blessing of all her earthly promises. The Temple will be rebuilt and animal sacrifices reinstated. These will serve as a reminder of the Old Testament sacrificial system; they will not achieve forgiveness of sins.

Those who teach this viewpoint always hold to a Pre-Tribulation Rapture of the Church. During the Tribulation the nation of Israel is converted (fulfilling Paul's words in Romans chapter 11 about all Israel being saved) and becomes the evangelist to the world.

All the objections that apply to historic Pre-Millennialism apply here also. However the additional objection would be that the Church is minimised through this teaching, as God's real agenda seems to be the nation of Israel. In effect the Old Testament is never superseded.

Post-Millennialism

Post-Millennialism teaches that there will be a golden age for the Church on earth before Christ returns. The 1000 years is symbolic of this golden age and it is Post-Millennial because Jesus returns *after* this time. During the 'Millennium' most of the world will become Christian. Many teach that the Tribulation is already over, having taken place during the time of the siege and destruction of Jerusalem in 70 AD. Some, however, would speak of an end-time apostasy. Jesus then returns and after the Final Judgement we immediately enter the eternal age.

Iain Murray gives the feel of Post-Millennialism in his book *The Puritan Hope*. He speaks of the Puritans looking for 'a period in the later days of the Church militant when under the special influence of the Holy Spirit, the spirit of the martyrs will appear again, true religion be greatly quickened and revived and the members of Christ's churches become so conscious of their strength in Christ that they shall to an extent unknown before, triumph over the power of evil both within and without'.[1]

A more extreme form of Pre-Millennialism known as Reconstructionism claims that the return of Christ will be so delayed that the Church will have time to take over national governments. This will not come about because of some Christian coup but simply because the Church is so successful in her mission that she will gain in influence to gradually take control in every area of life. Then society can be reconstructed according to the Bible and especially the Law of Moses.

Post-Millennialists will claim biblical support for their view from those verses which proclaim blessing for the Church and the advance of God's Kingdom. Jesus likened the Kingdom to a grain of mustard seed, which grows into a great tree whose branches fill the earth. Paul spoke of the full number of the Gentiles coming in (Romans 11:25). A key verse is 1 Cor 15:25: 'For he must reign until he has put all his enemies under his feet.'

So it has been said, 'I hold to Post-Millennialism not because I look at the world, but because I look at the Bible. And the Bible tells me all things shall be put under Christ's feet before the end.'

The main criticism of this viewpoint is that it is simply too optimistic. Where does scripture make it really clear that most of the world will become Christian? Also there are many scriptures which indicate pressure for the Church before the end and the love of many growing cold. Far from suggesting that the Tribulation is over, it is an event that is surely still to take place.

However, one can certainly state that the view is a stimulus to world mission for it encourages hopes of success and advance. It stands against a 'remnant theology' that would teach that we should expect decline in the Church before Christ returns: there will always be a faithful remnant, but we can't look for more than that. Post-Millennialism speaks of growth, not remnants.

A-Millennialism

A-Millennialism places an emphasis on the reign of Christ right now and is therefore sometimes referred to as Realised Millennialism. The 1000 years of Revelation is seen as a long period of time referring to the whole Church age during which Christ reigns from heaven. At the end of the age Jesus will return, the Church will be raptured, and the final judgement will then take place followed by the eternal age.

A-Millennialists tend to be pessimistic about the Church. They expect things to get worse, not better, and foresee the Church being reduced to a remnant of true believers who will be rescued by Christ when he returns.

The main objection to A-Millennialism has to do with the interpretation of Revelation chapter 20. A-Millennialists will claim to make a clear authentic interpretation of this chapter, but this is certainly challenged.

At the beginning of Revelation chapter 20 we read that Satan is locked and sealed in the Abyss for the 1000 years, unable to deceive the nations during that time. That hardly seems to square with the terrible things that have taken place in nations over the last 1900 to 2000 years, or to take note of the fact that certain North African nations, for example, which were once predominantly Christian, are now clearly Muslim. Satan does appear to have deceived nations during the Church age.

There is also a lot of technical discussion around the phrase 'came to life' in verses 4 and 5. Those who argue against A-Millennialism criticise an interpretation of that phrase which make it mean two different things. There are A-Millennialists who claim it means conversion in verse 4 and resurrection of the body in verse 5. Surely the same phrase (one word in Greek) cannot mean two different things in the space of two sentences. But other A-Millennialists interpret this passage of Revelation to refer to resurrection after death on both occasions. So the score seems about even on this point!

Can we simplify the issues? I believe we can. Essentially, if we cut away all the rather extreme views and speculations on this subject, we are faced with the central question of whether or not Christ will rule on the earth with his Church for 1000 years. I leave aside Post-Millennialism as impossibly optimistic as judged by the word of God, and surely incorrect when it states that the Tribulation is over and there is no more Big Trouble to come.

So we could anticipate the future to be like this. The Church will pass through the Tribulation. Christ will return and rapture his Church. Descending to the earth he will reign here for 1000 years and it will be a millennium of peace, blessing and prosperity. At the end of that time, Satan, who has been locked up during the Millennium, will be released and stir up a final rebellion. This will be destroyed by fire from heaven. Final Judgement will then take place followed by the eternal age.

Or we could argue that sometime in the future the Church will enter the Tribulation, with Satan stirring up a final great rebellion. Jesus will then return and rapture his Church. Immediately the final judgement takes place followed by the eternal age.

With either viewpoint there are some problems that are not easily overcome. Personally I tend towards the A-Millennial view, though with a rather more optimistic outlook than is typical. Surely the New Testament teaches that before the end there will be increasing difficulties, tribulation and persecution. Yet equally the New Testament promises that Christ will build his Church, the fullness of the Gentiles will come in, all Israel will be saved, the kingdom or government of God will advance and the gospel will reach every people group. Then the end will come (see Matt 24:14).

For me there is such a conviction about the apocalyptic nature of Revelation that I cannot easily accept Pre-Millennialism. We'll look at the book of Revelation later. Apocalyptic literature was well-known in the first century. It was a style of writing full of code, symbols and numbers. The reader had to understand the hidden message.

Therefore Revelation chapter 20 could be understood to refer to the situation of the Church during the whole period up to Jesus' return. There will be difficulties and persecutions. Martyred Christians appearing to lose all actually gain everything and reign with Christ in glory. The Church in heaven and on the earth waits, looking for the Return of Jesus, his final pronouncement of Judgement and the Eternal Age.

What about Satan being bound and unable to deceive the nations? That's the great problem for the A-Millennialist. Certainly Satan must be under some restraint right now, for the gospel does get out to the nations and tens of thousands are converted daily. Also we face this problem in other parts of the New Testament. In Colossians 2:15 we read, 'And having disarmed the powers and authorities, he made a public spectacle of them, triumphing over them by the Cross.' Yet despite such disarming Satan still seems very active in the world. The reality is that we live in a time between the defeat of Satan at the Cross and his destruction at the Return of Jesus. His power is presently limited, but certainly not spent.

But if I'm on earth for 1000 years longer than I expect, my Pre-Millennial friends will tell me how wrong I was as we enjoy a season of peace, joy, harmony and prosperity together.

Notes

1.   Iain H. Murray, *The Puritan Hope*, Banner of Truth, 1975.

5

What Happens When We Die?

We all have to die. Even Christians are reluctant to talk on this subject. We need to face the challenge of Paul's statement about death being gain for the believer. What happens to us at the moment of death? We will see that there is a difference between what is called the Intermediate state and the Final State. There could be a danger today that even Christians are resting too much of their hope of heaven on testimonies that are given to so-called after-death experiences. We need to see how this issue is clearly worked through in scripture, so that facing death ourselves then our hope will be secured on the promises of God.

What Happens When We Die?

Most of us are not keen to die. Yet the Bible tells us that to live is Christ and to die is gain for the believer (Phil 1:21). The Psalmist tells us, 'Blessed in the sight of the Lord is the death of his saints'. The Church where I am a Pastor was over ten years old before we lost our first member by death. In a church of 700 to 800 members that is quite a startling statistic. Here's another startling statistic: every member of my Church will die! The death rate will be 100 per cent in my Church.

Dying is the one thing we are certain to do ahead of Christ's return. Much as we may teach on prayer, discipling, generous giving or on the many other subjects relevant to the Christian life, to teach on death is to deal with the one subject that's going to affect everyone.

Sometimes people speak of a drop in the death rate. There's never a drop in the death rate! Death may be delayed, but finally it catches up with us all. In many churches today there is teaching on healing, and rightly so. But even healed people must eventually die. It is even more important therefore that we know what the Bible says about dying and death. Even the people that Jesus raised from the dead, sometime later died again. I've visited two tombs of Lazarus. One is in Bethany in Israel, supposedly the place where Jesus called him from the grave. The other is in a Greek Orthodox Church in Cyprus where legend tells us that Lazarus became a bishop. Whether or not either tomb is a genuine site, the point is made that the man Jesus raised four days after he died had at a later date to die again. We need to know what happens to us when we die.

Certainly, if we do not survive death then our Christianity is a waste of time. Worship is the highest call upon our lives. If we don't survive death, what is the point? We can't see God now and we will never see him. So what are we worshipping? If there is nothing beyond death then there was nothing for Jesus beyond death. We may sing 'Worthy is the Lamb' but there is no Lamb; he's dead and gone. Worship is pointless; we'd be better off doing something else on a Sunday morning.

If we don't survive death, why witness or why build the Church? Joining a club would probably be cheaper than paying our tithes to a local church. For those of us who are preachers our years of ministry would be a sheer waste of breath. We would be giving people false expectations and calling people to commit themselves to total unreality.

This is exactly how Paul argues it.

If there is no resurrection of the dead, then not even Christ has been raised. And if Christ has not been raised, our preaching is useless and so is your faith. More than that, we are then found to be false witnesses about God that he raised

Christ from the dead. But he did not raise him if the dead are not raised. For if the dead are not raised, then Christ has not been raised either. And if Christ has not been raised, your faith is futile; you are still in your sins. Then those also who have fallen asleep in Christ are lost. If only for this life we have hope in Christ, we are to be pitied more than all men. (1 Cor 15: 13–19)

Fortunately Paul adds in the next verse, 'But Christ has indeed been raised from the dead.'

We can't improve on Paul's logic. If we don't survive death then we are wasting our time. One thing makes sense of all we do as Christians – death is gain.

A failure to believe death is gain pushes everything into this life. We look here for all comfort or all security or the absolute need to have sexual experience, even if it is outside of a marriage relationship. Eat and drink for tomorrow we die – that says Paul, is the philosophy of the unbeliever. He believes in nothing beyond death, so grab what you can while you can. But even as believers we may wonder whether death will be loss for us rather than gain.

Paul is so confident of the gain of death for the believer that he even pictures himself in a struggle with a choice between staying in this life and going to be with Christ. Though his preference would be to go, he believes that by staying he can help the Church make progress and come to greater joy.

Why is it that we don't always share Paul's preference? Maybe it is largely to do with the pain of our loss when someone we know and love dies. Paul's letter to the Philippians is very helpful to us on this point. He is writing to thank the Church for a gift of money that has been brought to him by Epaphroditus, who is one of their church members. He'd nearly died when he visited Paul but the Apostle says that God had mercy on him, obviously referring to his recovery. But if death is gain as Paul claims in this same letter we might expect that the mercy of God would have been for Epaphroditus to die! However Paul speaks about being spared sorrow upon sorrow because of his recovery. So there was a challenge in death even for the Apostle Paul. It may be gain for the one who dies, but it is loss for us. We are left behind and are lonely. Our sense of loss can be so great that we can fail to grasp that death is gain.

So when a believer dies it's not just a matter of 'pulling ourselves together'. We can't expect to improve on the Apostle Paul's attitude. Even for him, facing the potential death of a friend would have been sorrow upon sorrow. Whatever the gain for the one who has died we have to cope with our loss. 'Brothers we do not want you to be ignorant about those who fall asleep, or to grieve like the rest of men who have no hope' (1 Thess 4.13). Our sure and certain hope is that they are with Christ – which is gain – and when our turn comes it will also be gain.

Providence and purpose

If death is such gain, then why don't we all want to die young? The answer is probably both Providence and Purpose. In the providence of God we seem to be wired to expect a lifespan of at least seventy years. This is just natural to us; it's the way we are made and anything less than seventy years seems a short life.

But we also have a purpose to our lives. Paul himself said he wished to depart and be with Christ, but he needed to stay for the benefit of the Church. This is true for all believers. As long as we stay we have a purpose in serving the Body of Christ and assisting its mission.

Death as gain

We should also consider what really are the gains of death for the believer.

Strangely, we never die. Jesus said, 'I am the resurrection and the life. He who believes in me will live, even though he dies; and whoever lives and believes in me will never die' (John 11:25,26). So believe in Jesus and though you die you will live. But, believe in Jesus and you will never die. It may seem a contradiction in words, but not in our spirit. When we die as believers we will live again, but as believers we never really die, we enter a better life; it is gain.

Imagine that you have always lived in a house with no windows. During the course of your life you move from room to room. Some rooms are poorly furnished, some quite comfortable and occasionally you spend time in one that is really luxurious. You are always aware that there is a back door to this house. It fascinates you, even makes you feel slightly nervous, for you wonder what is on the other side of the door. But one day you find yourself being irresistibly drawn to it with a mixture of excitement and nervousness. Suddenly the door swings open and you pass through and for the first time in your life you see lakes and trees, blue sky and sunshine. It is all gain. Death for the believer is only a door. We must go through it, but really we never die. It is all gain on the other side.

Have you ever thought that if death really is such gain then Lazarus may have missed out? We may picture the scene as Jesus called him from the grave. Martha and

Mary full of praise and wonder and possibly Lazarus himself shouting hallelujah! But he might have said, 'Why didn't you leave me when I was having such a good time?'

For the believer there is also a gain over troubles. Peter says, 'Now for a little while you may have had to suffer grief in all kinds of trials.' Certainly I have known believers for whom that would be a true description of their life. For those struggling with grief and trials it hardly seems like a little time. However what they gain will be forever.

Paul says that our 'light and momentary troubles are achieving for us an eternal glory that far outweighs them all.' Later in the same letter Paul gives a great catalogue of his sufferings as an Apostle, which hardly look light or momentary. But notice the contrasts that Paul draws. *Light* troubles compared with *weight* of glory. *Momentary* troubles compared with *eternal* glory. Death is gain. Whatever we face now (and Paul faced a great deal) it is to be superseded by such gain that Paul can dismiss present troubles as insignificant and passing.

There is also gain for us over present joys. Here is a real battleground. The reason we often want more in this life is because we may have our doubts about the next life. It can be hard to believe that it will all be better than now. Will it be better than my favourite holiday, or sport, or music, or sex? Paul makes it very personal: For me to live is Christ and to die is gain. It may be different, but it will always be better. We want to hold on to this life. We can even be driven to sin because we are looking for the better life now. But here and now is a pale shadow of life as it will be then. Beyond death delete the word heaven and insert the word *gain*.

There is even gain for God himself in the death of a believer. John Piper, drawing on Jonathan Edwards, reminds us that if God is the Supreme Being and the Highest Good in the universe, then it would be immoral if he did not focus on himself for his own joy and if he did not call us to set aside everything else to pursue him, for in him alone will be found our greatest joy. When we cross from this life to the next, God gains another perfect worshipper and we will find our supreme joy and happiness in the enjoyment of God himself.

At death

If death is such gain, then what happens to us immediately after we die?

Although we may claim not to fear death itself, we are aware that there is a door for us to go through, the other side of which we can only handle now in the realm of faith. We have not been there before.

Having said that, today, we not infrequently hear Christians' stories of after-death, or near-death experiences, all of which testify to the wonder of heaven. How do we handle these testimonies? Some doctors will seek to give a medical explanation for what takes place, claiming that supposed visions or experiences can be understood as the natural result of our brain closing down at death, followed by resuscitation. We also ought to be aware that the testimonies of some non-Christians who have a near-death experience seem very similar to a Christian's experience.

In the Bible we read of a number of people who certainly could have testified to after-death experiences. Jesus raised Jairus' daughter from death, the widow of Nain's son, and also Lazarus who had been in the tomb for four days. Surely Lazarus would have had quite a story! But we read not a word about their after-death experience.

I am certainly not suggesting that the stories we hear today are not authentic, but we must take care not to exalt testimony over scripture. When we come to the time of our death we cannot rely on a testimony of someone else's after-death experience, but rather on the promises of God's word. Perhaps the testimony that comes closest in the Bible to an after-death experience is Paul's 'out of the body' experience written in the third person. All commentators agree that the Apostle is speaking about himself when he says, 'I know a man in Christ who fourteen years ago was caught up in the third heaven. Whether it was in the body or out of the body I do not know – God knows. And I know that this man – whether in the body or apart from the body I do not know, but God knows – was caught up into paradise. He heard inexpressible things, things that man is not permitted to tell' (2 Cor 12:2–4).

It seems as if Paul, though given a glimpse of heaven, was actually unable to report on it!

Certainly, the fact that there is an appetite to devour testimonies of after-death experiences highlights the reality that death is an enemy. However, it is an enemy finally to be destroyed when Jesus comes again and brings in the fullness of his reign and rule. 'And I heard a loud voice from the throne saying, "Now the dwelling of God is with men, and he will live with them. They will be his people, and God himself will be with them and be their God. He will wipe every tear from their eyes. There will be no more death or mourning or crying or pain, for the old order of things has passed away"' (Rev 21:3,4).

Beyond Death

As the Apostle Paul was looking forward to what lies beyond death, let's probe what the Bible says about the death of a believer and a non-believer. The simple approach seems to be that the believer goes to heaven and the non-believer to hell. However that is in a way a simplistic approach.

It is important to understand that there is a distinction between death and final judgement in that they occur at different times, unless you are still alive when Jesus returns. Very commonly the New Testament speaks of the death of a Christian in terms of sleep. A clear example of this is the death of the first Christian martyr, Stephen. 'While they were stoning him, Stephen prayed, "Lord Jesus, receive my spirit." Then he fell on his knees and cried out, "Lord do not hold this sin against them." When he had said this, he fell asleep. And Saul was there, giving approval to his death' (Acts 7:59–8:1). So although Stephen is described as falling asleep it is abundantly clear from the passage that he dies. The New Testament never describes the death of a non-believer in terms of falling asleep.

Some have suggested a doctrine of what is called 'soul sleep', meaning that the Christian sleeps at death with no consciousness until the return of Christ. He will then be awakened from unconsciousness by the blast of the trumpet of God and the cry of the archangel. The Christian rises with a reawakened body and spirit to meet the Lord in the air. However, scripture seems to be against this idea, indicating rather an immediate consciousness at death for the Christian.

Jesus said to the dying and repentant thief, 'Today you

will be with me in paradise' (Luke 24:43). And we have already noted the verses that speak of Paul desiring to be with Christ and preferring to be away from the body and at home with the Lord. In the parable of Lazarus and the rich man, both are held in a state of consciousness after death, albeit in rather different places.

But if the believer is immediately with Christ after death, why is he described as sleeping? This is exactly what his body does. At death the body of a Christian sleeps, awaiting the resurrection, which will take place when Jesus returns. 'But our citizenship is in heaven. And we eagerly await a Saviour from there, the Lord Jesus Christ, who by the power that enables him to bring everything under his control, will transform our lowly bodies so that they will be like his glorious body' (Phil 3:20,21).

Also we read in John's words, 'Dear friends, now we are children of God, and what we will be has not yet been made known. But we know that when he appears, we shall be like him, for we shall see him as he is' (1 John 3:2).

So at death the body of the Christian sleeps, awaiting Christ's return when it will be raised up and transformed into the likeness of Jesus' own resurrection body, but the spirit of the Christian is immediately released to enjoy the company of Jesus. Theologians refer to this as 'the intermediate state' and it is most helpful, perhaps, to speak of the Christian's spirit being in Paradise, although to speak of the Christian who has died as being in heaven certainly conveys the idea that they are right now with the Lord.

Jesus said to the dying thief that he would be with him in Paradise that very day and when Paul describes his out of the body experience to the Corinthians he speaks of being caught up to the 'third heaven' and to Paradise.

The Westminster Confession refers to the intermediate

state in these words: 'The souls of the righteous being then made perfect in holiness and received into the highest heaven where they behold the face of God in light and glory, waiting for the full redemption of their bodies.'

The intermediate state and the final state of the believer are also indicated in 1 Thessalonians chapter 4. Paul says, '. . . we believe that God will bring with Jesus those who have fallen asleep in him' (v. 14). But in verse 16 he says, 'the dead in Christ will rise first'. So on the one hand we have believers coming with Christ at his return and on the other hand being raised up to meet him on his return. This apparent contradiction is resolved when we understand that the spirits of believers will accompany Jesus to be reunited with their risen bodies at Christ's return. We will then be as we are now, body and spirit but without the limitations of our present fleshly bodies as these will have been transformed to be like Jesus in his risen body. So in new bodies we will live forever in a new heavens and a new earth.

The Christian in the intermediate state or Paradise when he dies is therefore awaiting a final state that will come with the re-embodiment of the spirit.

What about those who die as non-believers? They also will experience an intermediate state, for their bodies will be raised at the return of Christ for final judgement. 'Do not be amazed at this, for a time is coming when all who are in their graves will hear his voice and come out – those who have done good will rise to live, and those who have done evil will rise to be condemned' (John 5:28,29). These words of Jesus are similar to a statement of Paul's on the same subject, '. . . I have the same hope in God as these men, that there will be a resurrection of both the righteous and the wicked' (Acts 24:15).

It is clear that the unredeemed will also be raised for final judgement – though what these unglorified bodies will look like the Bible does not tell us. But the intermediate state of such people before the final judgement takes some teasing out of the biblical material. It appears to be like this. In the Old Testament all the dead are consigned to Sheol. Nothing particularly good or bad seems to happen there, but it is a place of waiting, rather like a doctor's waiting room where you could be uncertain as to whether you will receive good news or bad news!

The New Testament translation of Sheol is Hades, not hell. The Greek word for hell is Gehenna, which is the place of final condemnation. Although there are occasional hints in the Old Testament that there was something more glorious to come for the people of God beyond Sheol, it is only when we come into the New Testament there is a developed understanding of life beyond death. Strictly we could say that all go to Hades after death, just as the Old Testament sees all in Sheol after death. But now Hades can be thought of as dividing into two with the spirits of the redeemed being in Paradise awaiting the return of Jesus and their resurrection bodies. The spirits of the unredeemed are held awaiting their final judgement.

When Jesus returns and all come before the great white throne, judgement is passed and the eternal state of both the redeemed and unredeemed begins in either heaven or hell. It is to the subject of judgement that we must turn in the next chapter.

6

All Up Before the Judge

No one who has ever lived can avoid the judgement of God. Whatever a person may have been in this life, he or she will have to stand in line with everyone else before the great white throne of judgement. Christians need to understand that their lives will also be assessed, the result of which will lead to a gain or loss of reward, though never to a loss of salvation. So to stimulate us to live zealous and faithful lives for God we will see there is grace, purpose for our lives and the promise of reward.

All Up Before the Judge

The judgement to come is the goal towards which all history and all mankind are moving. Judgement is an appointment no person who has lived on the earth can miss. God, the righteous judge, will demonstrate his perfect character as he pronounces acquittal or condemnation. There will be a vindication both of Jesus Christ and his Church. The old order will come to an end, the new order will begin. The dividing line between the two will be the day of judgement.

In the Old Testament there is much teaching on judgement. God executes his judgement on the nations and also on Israel in her sin. The destruction of Northern Israel by the Assyrians and Southern Judah by the Babylonians are both seen as the outworking of the judgement of God upon an apostate nation. Leon Morris says that in the Old Testament what we read of the judgements of God 'implied a passion for right'.

The theologian Oscar Cullman speaks of the coming judgement as 'the primary eschatological function of the

Son of Man'. It will affect all men and all nations. It will include the living and the dead, the good and the bad, believers and unbelievers. Jesus Christ will be the central and presiding figure on the day of judgement.

I'll give a brief overview of judgement as we find it in the New Testament; we ought to note particularly how it should influence the present lives of Christian believers.

Jesus taught it

First of all we should see that Jesus Christ himself taught persistently on this theme of judgement. To illustrate this here are a few verses on the subject taken from Matthew's gospel.

> Not everyone who says 'Lord, Lord' will enter the kingdom of heaven . . . I will tell them plainly, 'I never knew you.' (Matt 7:21–23)

> Do not be afraid of those who kill the body but cannot kill the soul. Rather, be afraid of the one who can destroy both body and soul in hell. (Matt 10:28)

In Matthew chapter 11 Jesus pronounces woes on various cities, concluding with these words, 'But I tell you it will be more bearable for Sodom on the day of judgement than for you.'

In chapter 25 Jesus gives us the parable of the sheep and goats, making clear that the two will be forever separated on the final day of judgement.

Our relationship to Jesus now will be the decisive issue on the day of judgement, for it is not possible to be right with God and wrong with Jesus. A vague belief in the existence of God will not deliver men and women from condemnation and loss. We need to be related to God who became flesh and lived, died and rose again on the earth, which means being related to Jesus Christ. 'Moreover, the Father judges no one, but has entrusted all judgement to the Son, that all may honour the Son just as they honour the Father. He who does not honour the Son does not honour the Father, who sent him' (John 5:23,23). There are other scriptures that also tell us that Jesus is the one who will act as judge at his coming. 'He commanded us to preach to the people and to testify that he (Jesus) is the one whom God appointed as judge of the living and the dead' (Acts 10:42). Again we see that it is Jesus who will exercise this supreme authority when Paul announces, 'For he has set a day when he will judge the world with justice by the man he has appointed. He has given proof of this to all men by raising him from the dead' (Acts 17:71).

With any rejection of Jesus Christ as Saviour and Lord there is a present aspect to judgement, 'Whoever believes in him is not condemned, but whoever does not believe stands condemned already because he has not believed in the name of God's one and only son' (John 3:18). However, such a present condemnation can only be regarded as partial and provisional and will one day merge into the full judgement of God when Jesus comes again. One of the most sobering verses in scripture must be Revelation 12:12, 'And I saw the dead great and small, standing before the throne, and the books were opened. Another book was opened, which is the book of life. The dead were judged according to what they had done as recorded in the book.' On that final awesome day of judgement people whom no one really knew on earth will stand alongside kings and slaves will stand beside dictators. But none will then have their rank recognised above another, all will stand open and vulnerable before the risen Christ to have their lives examined and for judgement to be pronounced. This is well captured in a passage from a sermon preached by Dr Martyn Lloyd Jones after the death of King George VI.

Death is the great leveller. We all have to face death; none are exempt from death. What you saw as headlines in your newspapers last Wednesday will soon be said of you. The heading was 'The King is Dead'. The day is coming when someone will turn to somebody else and say that about you. Death is the great leveller that brings us all to the same position. We are all equal at that point, there is no precedence at this point. Kings, and the highest in authority, here take their place with all others. We come face to face with God who is 'the King of kings and the Lord of lords'. The great question is, not how do we face this life and world, but how do we face death, how do we face eternity, how do we face God, how can we stand in the presence of His Majesty? And we are reminded here that there is but one way. The King of Heaven came down to earth, in order that you and I might be delivered from our sins, in order that the terrors of hell and of God with us 'might have nothing to do', in order that the books of Heaven might be cleared and we might become the children of God, in order that we might be delivered from every fear, the fear of death and the fear of judgement, the fear of the law and the fear of God in that terrifying sense, in order that we might be made meet to live in His presence. Thank God that as we therefore look into the face of death together this morning, we can do so without terror and without alarm because we know the King of kings is our Lord and Saviour, and He has opened up a new and living way, even through His broken body and His shed blood, into Heaven itself for us.[1]

Men and women may not like the idea of judgement and may claim to be atheist and therefore scornful of any prospect of judgement; but it is inescapable. The writer to the Hebrews says, 'Just as man is destined to die once, and after that to face judgement . . .' (Heb 9:27).

The outcome of the final judgement for unbelievers will be discussed in the chapter on hell, but we need to understand here that there is a judgement, though I prefer the term assessment, which Christians must also face. 'Judgement according to works is declared with sharp and sustained accents (in the New Testament) and we must simply listen with deep earnestness' (Berkouwer). Here are some scriptures that support this statement:

> For the Son of Man is going to come in his Father's glory with his angels, and then he will reward each person according to what he has done. (Matt 16:27)

> God will give to each person according to what he has done. (Rom 2:6)

> Since you call on a Father who judges each man's work impartially, live your lives as strangers here in reverent fear. (1 Pet 1:17)

> Behold, I am coming soon! My reward is with me, and I will give to everyone according to what he has done. (Rev 22:12)

Of course, the great emphasis of evangelical churches is the doctrine rediscovered at the time of the Reformation that a person is justified by faith and not by works. Yet scripture undoubtedly makes clear that all men, including those justified by faith, will face a judgement of their works.

Another scripture that brings this out as clearly as any is when Paul writes to the Corinthians, 'For we must all appear before the judgement seat of Christ, that each one may receive what is due to him for the things done while in the body, whether good or bad' (2 Cor 5:10). This is in a passage which without any question is being written to Christians and indeed goes on to assert, 'God made him who had no sin to be sin for us, so that in him we might become the righteousness of God' (2 Cor 5:21). This latter verse allows us to affirm in the words of Paul, 'there is therefore no condemnation for those who are in Christ Jesus' (Rom 8:1) but it does not allow us to claim there is therefore no judgement to face. There will be a judgement, or assessment, made of the way we have lived our lives as Christians and although this judgement cannot lead us to condemnation, it can lead us to loss.

We can find at least three stimuli in Scripture for Christians to live faithful and zealous lives.

Grace

Paul puts it explicitly for us when he says, 'For the grace of God that brings salvation has appeared to all men. It teaches us to say "No" to ungodliness and worldly passions, and to live self-controlled, upright and godly lives in this present age' (Titus 2:11,12). The inherent danger of the Bible's message of grace is that we become what is called 'antinomian', or against the law. If salvation is all of God, what does it matter how I live? I cannot save myself, my good works will never achieve redemption, and I am saved by grace alone. But rightly understood, if God has taken such a wonderful initiative in our lives and freely given us a salvation that we certainly do not deserve, then really our response should be, how can I fully live my life in gratitude to God for this great salvation?

John Piper has made the point that although gratitude to God for saving us in the past can certainly be understood as a motivation for present Christian behaviour, the Bible itself tends to motivate by what he calls, Future Grace. 'Everyone who has this hope in him (the hope of Christ's return in the future) purifies himself, just as he is pure' (1 John 3.3).

Purpose

God has chosen and saved us for a purpose that is described three times in Ephesians chapter 1 as living for the praise of his glory. Our purpose in life is not to discover the purpose in life, but to live in a way that pleases God. Undoubtedly this includes good works and the Bible is specific on this: 'For it is by grace you have been saved, through faith – and this not from yourselves, it is the gift of God – not by works, so that no one can boast. For we are God's workmanship, created in Christ Jesus to do good works, which God prepared in advance for us to do' (Eph 2:8–10). There is a danger in the Christian life that I can become bored and simply drift along. In fact God has saved us to do good works. We're here for a purpose, not for a rest!

Reward

This is the stimulus that bears most directly on the issue of judgement. The way we live out our Christian life now will have an effect on loss or gain of reward as we enter heaven. The most explicit passage on this subject (though we have already noted several scriptures that talk of a judgement of our works) is found in 1 Corinthians chapter 3. We are urged to take care how we build our lives on the foundation of Christ. On the day of judgement our works will be tested by fire, either to be destroyed or remain. For the one whose work survives the test there will be reward, but for the one whose work is burned up he will, in Paul's memorable statement, 'suffer loss; he himself will be saved, but only as one escaping through the flames' (1 Cor 3:15). This assures us that there can be no loss of our salvation, but it warns us that there can be loss of reward.

What rewards can be lost or gained? I suggest that the Bible hints at certain things rather than being very specific.

There is the matter of the welcome we shall receive as we enter glory. 'Therefore, my brothers, be all the more eager to make your calling and election sure. For if you do these things, you will never fall, and you will receive a rich welcome into the eternal kingdom of our Lord and Saviour Jesus Christ' (2 Peter 1:10,11). The fact that we can receive a rich welcome suggests that we could receive a poor welcome.

Also we can recall from the parables of Jesus that there will be those who will rule over a greater or lesser number of cities. There must be some use of picture language here, nevertheless it does hint at different levels of responsibility in eternity. We may feel the better reward would be less responsibility, but clearly in eternal glory this would be responsibility without pressure. Even in a perfect creation before the Fall, Adam was charged with the commission to subdue the earth and rule over the animal kingdom. There must be something equivalent to this responsibility in a new heavens and earth.

There is also a promise of a crown held out to those who do well. The letters of Revelation speak of a crown of life, Timothy is reminded that there is a crown of righteousness to be awarded, and Peter speaks of a crown of glory. It seems unlikely that these are literal crowns that will balance one on another, but they can be understood as symbolic of future reward.

I sometimes speak with those who confess themselves to be uneasy about working for eternal reward; it seems somehow more spiritual to determine to work hard with no promise of reward. But we do well not to try and improve upon the Bible! The Corinthians were instructed, '. . . Run in such a way as to get the prize. Everyone who competes in the games goes into strict training. They do it to get a crown that will not last; but we do it to get a crown that will last forever. Therefore I do not run like a man running aimlessly; I do not fight like a man beating the air. No, I beat my body and make it my slave so that after I have preached to others, I myself will not be disqualified for the prize' (1 Cor 9:24–27).

If it's good enough for Paul to press on for a prize it should be good enough for us. He also says to the Philippians, 'I press on towards the goal to win the prize for which God has called me heavenwards in Christ Jesus' (Phil 3:14). And in the next verse he adds, 'All of us who are mature should take such a view of things' We do well to press on in the Christian life, looking for reward, not risking loss, as we enter glory.

Notes

1. Martyn Lloyd Jones, taken from a leaflet at his Memorial Service.

7

Heaven on Earth

To understand heaven we need to recognise both what will happen to our bodies and what will happen to our planet. We shall receive new bodies and we shall live on a new earth. Typically, we can be too vague about the subject of heaven, simply thinking of it as up there, out there, somewhere. A clearer appreciation of the tangible nature of our bodies and of where we are to live for eternity as well as what we might be doing should help us to become more excited about our future.

Heaven on Earth

Christian believers today can often be heard discussing power, healing and miracles, but not often be heard discussing death and heaven. Why are we so reluctant to discuss the afterlife?

Perhaps it's because we think that heaven will be one long church service. Depending on your view of church services that may not always be too exciting a prospect. Heaven also suffers from a cartoon image. It's often represented in terms of disembodied spirits or angel-like creatures that now flit from cloud to cloud twanging golden harps on a kind of endless Bank Holiday. The many jokes about Peter greeting people at the pearly gates of heaven hardly raise our excitement levels either. Again, even if not admitted, Christians may wonder whether there is something rather undesirable about heaven. The Sadducees once asked Jesus about a woman who'd married seven times, losing each husband by death. The question was whom she would be married to in heaven. Jesus replied there would be no marriage in heaven. That can be interpreted as disappointing or even dull!

We live in the age of the instant. We even have the possibility of buying a lottery scratch card and instantly winning £50,000. To talk of heaven is to speak of a future and, many probably wish, a distant hope. We have a life to live now. There is a mortgage or rent to be paid. There is a job to obtain or a career to be managed right now. Heaven is too far off, it's too pie in the sky when we die. We may even be aware that in past centuries the slaves on plantations were sometimes taught not to be concerned about their present terrible and fearful condition, but to look to the hope of being with Jesus in heaven. That seems a dreadful blasphemy when such people were in the most desperate need of help and release from their cruel exploitation. To seek to comfort them with thoughts of heaven in the future was no way to overlook their current situation.

So there are several reasons why Christians may be reluctant to speak of the delights that await us beyond death – indeed, how often in these days do we hear sermons preached on heaven rather than just references to eternal life?

By contrast, the Apostle Paul was a man thinking about heaven and excited by its prospects: 'For me to live is Christ and to die is gain.' Also, 'I desire to depart and be with Christ, which is better by far' (Phil 1:21,23).

The Apostle also writes to the Corinthians: 'We are confident, I say, and would prefer to be away from the body and at home with the Lord' (2 Cor 5:8). Also we should not overlook Paul's account of a 'visit' to heaven, which though cast in the third person is clearly a testimony to his own experience. 'I know a man in Christ who fourteen years ago was caught up to the third heaven.

Whether it was in the body or out of the body I do not know – God knows. And I know that this man – whether in the body or apart from the body I do not know, but God knows – was caught up to paradise. He heard inexpressible things, things that man is not permitted to tell' (2 Cor 12:2–4). Even in these rather mysterious verses one senses a barely restrained excitement about heaven in the Apostle's writing and thinking.

In order properly to understand heaven we first need to understand something about ourselves and the new bodies that we are going to receive. It doesn't matter what we believe about the timing of the Rapture and the Tribulation, all Christians will receive a new body when Jesus returns.

> For the Lord himself will come down from heaven, with a loud command, with the voice of the archangel and with the trumpet call of God, and the dead in Christ will rise first. After that, we who are still alive and are left will be caught up together with them in the clouds to meet the Lord in the air. And so we will be with the Lord forever. (1 Thess 4:16,17)

These verses tell us that, when Christ comes again, those who have died as Christians will be raised up to meet Christ in the air, to be followed immediately by those who are still alive as Christians. The question that then arises is what kind of shape we will all be. This is relevant both for those who have previously died and those who are still alive. As far as the multitudes of dead Christians are concerned, they are not only raised but also given new bodies, which will be like Christ's own glorious body.

> But our citizenship is in heaven. And we eagerly await a saviour from there, the Lord Jesus Christ, who by the power

that enables him to bring everything under his control, will transform our lowly bodies so that they will be like his glorious body. (Phil 3:20,21)

Exactly the same teaching about the body is given in 1 John 3:2 and 1 Corinthians 15:49.

As for those who are still alive when Jesus returns, and therefore do not need their bodies to be raised up, they will nevertheless be totally transformed, also into the likeness of the risen Jesus. 'Listen, I tell you a mystery: we will not all sleep but we will be changed – in a flash, in the twinkling of an eye, at the last trumpet. For the trumpet will sound, the dead will be raised imperishable and we will be changed' (1 Cor 15:51,52).

It is understandable that other issues begin to come to our minds when we consider this teaching. What about those Christians who have died without trace? There are Christians whose bodies have been destroyed in war, and indeed cremation is more common for Christians today than burial. Paul anticipates such questions, again in 1 Corinthians 15. 'But someone may ask, "How are the dead raised? With what kind of body will they come?"' (v. 35). Paul's immediate reply is something of a put-down, 'How foolish!' (v. 36), as though we shouldn't ask such questions at all. Fortunately, realising our limited understanding on these matters, the Apostle does go on to give us an answer. He argues that our bodies are just like seed. Put a seed into the ground; it can be like a speck of dust that simply disappears in that form but grows up to produce a plant just as God has determined. So we may be reduced to mere dust, but God has a purpose for us and he will miraculously raise us up with new, resurrection bodies.

This is a very encouraging doctrine. For those of us

who really don't like the way we look now, the good news is that we are going to radically improve! It is genuinely a wonderful prospect for Christians who are presently physically handicapped; they will find a release, not simply through death, but into the liberty of a new resurrection body.

Jesus came to this world like us. The incarnation means that Jesus took on human flesh. But we are going to become like him when he returns to collect us from the earth.

Let's turn next to consider the nature of heaven itself. There is a fairly common view among Christians today that the Bible is almost completely silent on the subject. This may arise from a quotation given in 1 Corinthians 2:9, 'However, as it is written: "No eye has seen, no ear has heard, no mind conceived what God has prepared for those who love him"'. So the argument is that we cannot know about heaven, we simply haven't been told. But the above quotation receives a comment in the very next verse of Paul's writing, 'but God has revealed it to us by his spirit' (1 Cor 2:10). We cannot claim that right now we know everything there is to know about heaven; after all, we've already seen that in Paul's own 'out of the body' experience he heard things that he was not permitted to tell. Clearly though, there is some Biblical revelation for us. There are descriptions that we can confidently give of the nature of heaven.

If, as we have seen, we are going to receive risen, transformed and glorified bodies then we will need somewhere to live. To say we will live in heaven, though true, can be too vague – we will live on a transformed and glorified earth! This can sound like the teaching of Jehovah's Witnesses but too often we may simply be living in negative reaction to what they say at our doors. The Witnesses claim that 144,000 will go to heaven and the rest of the Witnesses will live on earth. We typically respond by declaring that all Christians will go to heaven. But then we can be rather vague as to what we really mean by heaven. It's up there, out there somewhere! In fact, the consistent teaching of the New Testament is that the Christ who will transform our lowly bodies at his return will also transform our decaying planet; indeed he will transform the whole created universe.

The Bible speaks repeatedly of a new heaven and a new earth.

In the Old Testament we see it in the prophecy of Isaiah, 'Behold, I will create new heavens and a new earth. The former things will not be remembered, nor will they come to mind' (Isa 65:17).

Paul speaks of the hope of it. 'The creation waits in eager expectation for the sons of God to be revealed. For the creation was subjected to frustration, not by its own choice, but by the will of the one who subjected it, in hope that the creation itself will be liberated from its bondage to decay and brought into the glorious freedom of the children of God' (Rom 8:19–21).

Peter prophesies it again, 'But in keeping with his promise we are looking forward to a new heaven and a new earth, the home of righteousness' (2 Peter 3:13). The promise referred to here is of course the one quoted above in the prophecy of Isaiah.

In the Book of Revelation John is given a vision of the end and he sees all that is promised elsewhere in scripture finally fulfilled, 'Then I saw a new heaven and a new earth, for the first heaven and the first earth had passed away . . .' (Rev 21:1).

Some may wonder why there is a need for a new heaven. The word heaven is used in different ways in the Bible. There are occasions when it means the dwelling place of God; there are other times when it refers to the sun, moon, stars and planets. It's always obvious from the context which is the right understanding. If the word 'earth' is being used simply to describe the object of God's creation that we live on, then when used in conjunction with the word 'heavens' the latter must refer to the rest of the created universe.

Also there is some discussion about the way we should understand the earth to be made new. I prefer to speak of a *renewed* earth. Comparing the various relevant scriptures it would appear that this earth will not be totally destroyed but rather completely purified by fire from which conflagration there emerges a transformed earth. Just as we will continue to exist in eternity with new bodies, so this earth will continue in eternity, but totally renewed.

In the Book of Revelation the writer gives us a clear picture of a merger taking place between heaven (the dwelling place of God) and the earth, so that in effect they become one. 'I saw the Holy City, the new Jerusalem, coming down out of heaven from God, prepared as a bride beautifully dressed for her husband. And I heard a loud voice from the throne saying, "Now the dwelling of God is with men, and he will live with them . . ."' (Rev 21:2–3, see also Rev 21:9,10).

At one level the picture of a city dressed as a Bride is a very peculiar one. However the symbolism is clear enough to any student of the Bible. What we have here is the Church, the Bride of Christ, in all her glory coming to live upon the earth. God himself is living among his people. Heaven has come to earth; earth has become heaven.

Any action?

Finally, let's consider what we may be doing in heaven. At the beginning of this chapter I stated that Christians appear reluctant to talk very much on this subject. Perhaps many fear a lack of any exciting activity in heaven. Eternal life does last a very long time! And even if one projects into heaven the possibility of engaging in our favourite earthly activities, contemplate doing that forever and we could wonder if it might become awesomely boring. How many people look forward to an annual holiday with great excitement, only to return after 2–3 weeks, having enjoyed it but glad to be home again. It's nice to go travelling, but . . .!

There can be no prospect that in eternity, time will somehow hang heavy on us. Wayne Grudem describes time and eternity like this:

> . . . there will still be a succession of moments one after another and things happening one after another in heaven. We will experience eternal life not in an exact duplication of God's attribute of eternity, but rather in a duration of time that will never end: we, as God's people, will experience fullness of joy in God's presence for all eternity – not in the sense that we will no longer experience time, but in the sense that our lives with him will go on forever.[1]

David Pawson helpfully gives us a list of 7 S's and 7 R's which help us to understand what happens in heaven.[2]

Seven things not present in heaven:

1. *Sex*   Because there is no marriage.
2. *Suffering* There will be no more death or pain (Rev 21:4)

3. *Separation*   In Revelation 21:1 we read there will no longer be any sea in the new heavens and earth. To the Jews the sea represented separation.

4. *Sorrow*   Every tear is wiped away (Rev 21:4).

5. *Shadows*   Heaven is not lit by sun or moon but is incandescent with the glory of God (Rev 21:23).

6. *Sanctuary*   There is no Temple in heaven; for God himself is the temple (Rev 21:22).

7. *Sin*   Nothing impure can enter heaven (Rev 21:27).

Seven things we will find in heaven:

1. *Reward*   We looked at this in the last chapter.

2. *Responsibility*   We shall even judge the angels and be stewards of what will be Paradise restored on earth. Adam and Eve were told to oversee a perfect creation; so will we.

3. *Revelation*   We'll no longer see things dimly; we shall understand (1 Cor 13:12).

4. *Recognition*   Eternal life is meaningless unless I consciously continue to exist. If I know I still exist I shall surely recognise others as well. On the Mount of Transfiguration Moses and Elijah were recognisable even by disciples who'd never met them!

5. *Righteousness*   This will be the air of heaven (2 Pet 3:13).

6. *Rejoicing*   It begins with the wedding supper of the Lamb, but will go on forever.

7. *Rest*   From weariness, but not activity.

I would make two additions to this list.

Heaven will surely be an immensely *social* place. We read in Revelation chapter 7 of the vast crowd of the redeemed drawn from every people group that stand together before the throne of God. Apostles will mingle with children from Africa. Chinese martyrs will mix with American evangelists. However, what we were will be of no significance; we will be united in perfect fellowship, one people purchased by Christ.

Unlimited *travel* will surely be possible. This is implied by the fact that we will have new bodies without the limitations of the present model! If we are to live in a restored Universe, a new heaven and a new earth, then it seems reasonable to suggest we will not be restricted to just one place, but will have the freedom to travel it all. The universe, presently so obviously dead as well as vast beyond our imagining, will live. We will have eternity to explore but never exhaust the riches of Christ that will make up his restored creation.

The present creation, as we view it, can only be a hint in a fallen world of what a restored creation will be like. Yet if we consider the marvels, beauty, wonder and majesty of the present fallen creation, what a universe will be opened up for us to explore.

Rather than argue too much about a millennium – a mere 1000 years – let's get excited about heaven that will last forever, on the earth.

Notes

1. Wayne Grudem, *Systematic Theology*, IVP, Downers Grove, Ill./Leicester, England, 1973, p. 173.
2. David Pawson, Series of tapes on the End Times.

8

The Burning Issue

Distasteful as it may be to us, we cannot avoid the subject of hell when talking about the end times. A doctrine that teaches that people could be punished forever because of their rebellion against God in this life does not find wide acceptance today. There are attempts made not only by non-Christians, but also by believers to find an acceptable alternative to the standard doctrine of hell. The most likely alternative is what is called Annihilationism, which while teaching the reality of hell also suggests that the punishment is finite and not eternal in duration. However there are serious challenges to such an alternative. Whatever our convictions about hell the doctrine should stir our zeal and our compassion to bring the gospel and the hope of heaven to all people.

The Burning Issue

From earliest times there has been the idea deep in human nature that after death there is a good place and a bad place which will reflect some kind of justice for the way we've lived in this life. Christians speak of heaven and hell, but if we're reluctant to talk about heaven, we're probably even more coy on the subject of hell.

A standard, orthodox, evangelical definition of hell could be expressed like this: 'A place and/or state of conscious separation from God where the wicked are punished forever'. If this is true, it should be terrifying, which is perhaps why even evangelical Christians can seem almost embarrassed about this teaching today.

There are of course plenty of objections to the possibility of hell's existence. Even non-Christians will protest that God is surely a God of love, how could he ever intentionally send anyone to eternal punishment, with the exception perhaps of Hitler and child murderers. We ought to note though that once you've agreed a hell for anybody, you have agreed to the possibility of its existence.

The argument will also be put that hell is simply not fair or moral. It is out of proportion to the crime to punish people forever. Also punishment should seek to help people reform their ways and start again; there's no hope of that in hell. Again, surely we shouldn't go around trying to frighten people – that's a terrible form of manipulation. Of course on this last point we could say that to frighten people about real danger may be healthy. We want small children to have a fear of traffic, not to boldly walk in front of fast moving cars.

As many Christian churches and indeed cults that claim biblical authority turn away from a doctrine of hell, it does remain within the theology of both Roman Catholics and Evangelicals, though even here perhaps with less conviction than there used to be.

Of course all those who deny the existence or reality of hell are faced with a tough question: doesn't this mean we are faced with an eternal injustice? No fear of punishment after death could encourage even more selfish and criminal behaviour in this life. The force of this is often accepted, and various suggestions are made. The two favourite seem to be that either hell is self-imposed in this life or that bad people are simply annihilated at death. Concerning the former, we witness something rather different. Not all evil people, however we judge that, do have a bad time now. Some live prosperous lives and long ones at that. By contrast, many whom we might consider real heroes of the faith have a tough life and an early death. To suggest that wicked people simply cease to exist after death could actually be quite an attractive option and indeed encourage ever more selfish behaviour. Eat and drink for tomorrow we die; so let's grab what we can while we can and if others get hurt, so what?

A Christian picking up his Bible to study this subject will find very little about it in the Old Testament. This is immediately a surprise, because the Old Testament is often regarded as the more severe part of the Bible. Many Christians have the idea that somehow God softens his style in the New Testament!

Paul wrote on the subject of punishment after death, but the person who talks about it most is Jesus himself. Again this may be a surprise. We rightly think of Jesus expressing love, care and compassion. However we find it is the Lord who teaches us about hell. There have sometimes been unwise attempts to construct two theologies in the New Testament; the one as expressed by Jesus and the other by Paul. That has been clearly demonstrated to be false, but for those attempting it there needs to be a reminder that the teaching of Jesus gives us the doctrine of hell.

It is quite common for evangelical preachers to underline the exclusive claims of Christ as the unique way to reconciliation with God by quoting his words to the disciples, 'I am the way and the truth and the life. No one comes to the Father except through me' (John 14:6). For our purpose here we need to see that Jesus is not only pointing to himself as the one way to God, but he is speaking the truth because he is the Truth. Therefore whatever Jesus said on the subject of hell must also be true otherwise we are forced to reject Jesus as the Truth.

The word that Jesus used for hell – 'Gehenna' – is the name of a deep valley outside Jerusalem. Today you can still walk through the valley for it is now a landscaped park, though considerably filled in from its original depth, having in the past been the rubbish tip for the city. As the local rubbish dump in the time of Jesus, and even the place where the bodies of executed criminals were thrown, it was full of worms or maggots and fires burned continually to consume the refuse.

We must refer to this again, but there is an important discussion over what it means to be 'destroyed'. In Matthew 10:28 we read, 'Do not be afraid of those who kill the body but cannot kill the soul. Rather, be afraid of the One who can destroy both soul and body in hell.' The Greek word for destroy is *apollumi* which is defined like this: 'the idea is not extinction but ruin, loss, not of being, but of well being' (W. E. Vine). In John 3:16 the same word is translated as 'perish': 'For God so loved the world that he gave his one and only son, that whoever believes in him shall not perish but have eternal life.' In English we sometimes use the word 'perish' to refer to something that has become utterly useless but is not utterly destroyed. A hot water bottle or a car tyre can perish; they still exist, but they are thrown out as useless rubbish. Therefore we can argue that to be destroyed in Gehenna is not to be annihilated but to be thrown there as useless rubbish.

The Bible describes hell in terms of judgement (Rev 20:11–15), fire (Matt 5:22), darkness (Matt 25:30), prison (1 Peter 3:19) and a second death (Rev 21:8). The Bible is equally clear about what it will be like to suffer in hell. From the gospels alone we learn that it will mean separation from God, misery and torment. The company will be that of the devil and demons. Hell will be eternal and it is a fixed and final state from which there is no removal or return or escape.

Alternative understanding of hell

We will now look at the alternatives that have been offered to the above description of hell, even by Christian believers. Can it really be possible that people, wicked though they may be, will have to endure forever the kind of misery we've just described?

Some people, while claiming to be Christian, would simply declare that a loving God would not send people to hell, so it does not in reality exist. A view taken on this subject, which adds up to everyone being saved, is known as universalism. This not only overlooks what the Bible clearly says, but also ignores the fact that love is not God's only attribute. All that God is springs from his total otherness, his holiness. Certainly God is love, but the Bible also speaks of the wrath of God against sin and against sinners.

Evangelical Christians would immediately declare that they are not universalists, because they believe the Bible. However it is sometimes difficult to really break free of the idea that a person in the end is saved by works. It's been said that we can all become universalists at the graveside. A person may never have professed any kind of Christian belief and never been a member of a local church, yet at the graveside there is the tendency to think of all their good points and perhaps assume that they'll be alright after all. I am not for one moment suggesting that we have the right to pronounce final judgement on a person; only God can do that. However we should not allow ourselves to imply in any way that surely such a person is now in heaven. This kind of subconscious universalism will blunt our witness to the gospel of Christ.

Another suggestion is that the unbeliever will be offered a second chance after death, though logically this ends up again in universalism. There is however an attempt to justify this position from the Bible.

For Christ died for sins once for all, the righteous for the unrighteous, to bring you to God. He was put to death in the body but made alive by the spirit, through whom also he went and preached to the spirits in prison who disobeyed long ago when God waited patiently in the days of Noah while the ark was being built. (1 Peter 3:18–20)

Two possible ways of interpreting the scripture again make it impossible to regard it as giving any credibility of a second chance after death. The word here used for preach is not *euangelizomai* (preach the gospel) but *kerusso*, which means 'proclaim'. Jesus did not preach the gospel to the spirits, he proclaimed his victory. But the other way of understanding this scripture is that the spirit of Jesus inspired Noah to preach to people who were disobedient in his own time and whose spirits are now held in prison awaiting final judgement. Peter has already, in the first chapter of this letter, spoken of the spirit of Christ in the prophets.

We know that Noah was a preacher of righteousness in his own day (2 Peter 2:5) and if Jesus did descend into the prison of departed spirits it would seem very odd indeed that he would preach only to those who died in the time of Noah.

For those who would ask, 'Did Jesus not descend into hell?' we could reply, 'Yes, certainly he did when he died at Calvary in our place, bearing our sin, guilt and punishment.'

Some Christians have favoured the idea of what is called conditional immortality. We are only given immortality on the condition that we believe in Jesus. Therefore the judgement that non-believers receive is their total extinction at death. It is hell, for it is separation from

God; it is total and it is everlasting. The debate centres on a verse in 1 Timothy 6:16 which refers to God alone being immortal. So either we have to say that God only gives immortality to believers or that although immortality only belongs inherently to God all men are made in God's image and therefore a man is an immortal being. Peter Lewis writes:

> It is true that the soul is immortal by nature, that immortality is an innate quality of the human soul is a Greek idea and not a biblical one. However we can claim the idea of immortality of the soul as a biblical one, and not merely a philosophical idea, if we are clear that immortality is a gift of creation (not simply of redemption) and is bound up with God's intention of what human beings should be. Hence, when God says, 'Let us make man in our image, after our likeness' (Gen 1:26) he is announcing a decision to share his own everlasting existence with men and women. Immortality then is intrinsic to what it is to be human in God's sight, and is a gift.[1]

Arguably, oblivion at death is immoral for it means that finally there is no justice and also a number of statements in scripture about eternal punishment are overlooked (e.g. Matt 25:46).

The most serious challenge to the orthodox view on hell comes from those who teach the doctrine of 'annihilationism'. Unlike conditional immortality this teaches that sinners survive death; they are held awaiting judgement, during which time the shocking consequences of their sin and eternal separation from God become starkly clear to them. They must face the judgement of God, but the final outworking of that judgement is annihilation. So annihilationism is not an easy option, but it does teach a limited and finite time to the sufferings of sinners.

The prominent Bible teacher John Stott inclines to this view and it has become a subject of major debate in recent years. Certainly Stott believes in banishment from God that will be real, terrible and eternal, but the question is, will it be everlasting suffering? Stott writes: 'Emotionally I find the concept intolerable and do not understand how people can live with it without either cauterising their feelings or cracking under the strain.'[2] He does acknowledge however that feelings are not to be regarded as our supreme authority as they are unreliable.

Some of the points that Stott makes are summarised here:

Language

Stott picks upon the word 'destruction' which we looked at above, and suggests that it is not possible to suffer destruction without actually being destroyed. He recognises that the word can be used in the sense of perishing (John 3:16) but it is difficult to imagine a perpetually inconclusive process of perishing.

He, too, agrees that immortality of the soul is a Greek and not a biblical concept and therefore cannot accept it is impossible for human beings to be totally destroyed.

Imagery

Stott puts a particular focus on fire. The main purpose of fire must be to destroy, not to cause pain. If the fire is eternal, then it would be odd if what was thrown into it was not destroyed.

Justice

God judges people according to what they have done (Rev 20:12). Conscious *eternal* torment seems to outweigh any amount of finite sin.

Universalism

The word is here used in a different sense to the way we used it earlier in this chapter. How can the universal victory of Christ be true if there still exists through all eternity millions who have been in rebellion to Christ and still remain separated from him?

Whether or not we agree with a doctrine of annihilationism the above points need to be taken seriously and cannot simply be brushed aside.

David Pawson's reply to the doctrine of annihilationism, in his book *The Road to Hell*, is particularly helpful with regard to the term 'everlasting'. He points out that the word 'everlasting' is used in Matthew chapter 25 to refer to fire and punishment as well as to life. We expect our life to go on forever, so the fire and the punishment must go on forever. However there are those who will argue that everlasting or eternal life has to do with a quality rather than a quantity of life. The truth is that it probably refers to both.

David Pawson says that one phrase beyond debate is the one translated 'for ever and ever'. This is the most emphatic phrase for endless time and is applied to hell. The annihilationist wants to argue that it is the punishment of hell that lasts forever, i.e. annihilation. But in fact the phrase 'for ever and ever' is used in the New Testament to describe the torment of hell (see Rev 14:11 and 20:10).

In conclusion the following points need to be noted on this subject.

1. Annihilationism is not standard, orthodox, evangelical belief. Roman Catholicism before the Reformation and Evangelical Christianity since the Reformation have regarded eternal punishment in hell as part of their standard doctrine.

2. Images of hell tend to put the emphasis on conscious physical pain, and this is what seems to be most intolerable for us to handle on this subject. Certainly the New Testament refers to body and soul being destroyed in hell (Matt 10:28). Perhaps, however, we should remember that as Christ took our place on the cross his experience also included darkness, thirst and a sense of total abandonment. In hell the unredeemed will be most conscious of darkness outside of Christ's light and glory with a thirst for God, which can now never be satisfied. There will be a sense of total abandonment. I don't want to make hell sound less than it is, but the New Testament itself hints at different degrees of hell. Some will be punished more severely than others (see Luke 12:47,48). In Romans chapter 2 Paul speaks of those who store up wrath against themselves. Again, this could be understood as indicating greater punishment for some than others.

3. We must be careful not to preach hell as though it is not too awful. David Pawson is right to point out that Jesus spoke mostly to his disciples about hell. That could imply that rather than constantly threaten the unbeliever, what we know about the terrors of hell should drive and motivate believers to an urgent

preaching and witness to the gospel by which men can be saved.

4. I once asked the well-known Bible teacher Michael Eaton how hell could exist in a restored creation, within the new heavens and new earth. He replied that he was not interested in philosophical questions, only in exegetical ones! He's right of course. We can continually be raising the philosophical questions and yet never receiving an answer. If the Bible teaches that there is an everlasting hell then the issue is settled.

5. By any definition, hell is eternal separation from God. We read that Whitefield and McCheyne preached on the subject with tears. Evangelicals today can almost preach it with glee, arrogant in our knowledge of the truth.

We can preach on hell because we believe it to be true, but our attitude may be pride in knowledge of the truth. Or we can preach on hell because we have compassion. There really is a hell to be avoided and a heaven to be won.

Notes

1.   Peter Lewis, *The Glory of Christ*, Moody Press, 1997, p. 445.
2.   John Stott, in *Essentials: A Liberal-Evangelical Dialogue*, Hodder & Stoughton, 1988, p. 314.

9

Can we get Revelation?

Many people feel the Book of Revelation is so difficult to understand that they don't even bother to read it. This leaves it open to the possibility of extreme and even sensational interpretations. There is a general consensus among evangelical scholars that although this book is set within the time frame of the 1st century Church and although it definitely has much to say about the end of this world's history, it is also a book that is entirely relevant to the Church in every generation. Fundamentally we are reading of the victory of God. Certainly the people of God will face great pressure, but God's triumph is certain. This book is always meant to lead us to praise and worship.

Can we get Revelation?

The Apostle John wrote the Book of Revelation during a period of exile on a treeless and rocky island called Patmos. It was probably written about 96 AD and therefore the last book of the Bible to be written.

Over the years labels have been attached to the different interpretations of the book. The Preterist view claims that the relevance of the prophecy lies in the immediate lifetime of the author and his readers. The Historicist view sees Revelation as giving a panoramic overview of history from the first century until the return of Christ. The Futurist interpretation sees the relevance of the book as being strictly for the end of the age whilst the Idealist view sees Revelation as a kind of poetic composition designed to convey to suffering Christians the inspiration to persevere.

Perhaps the best way to understand this book is to combine the best elements of all the above interpretations. The book is set within the historical framework of the early Church. It is a book that is relevant to every stage of church history. It does have prophetic statements to make about the end of the age. It is also a spiritual encourage- ment to Christians under pressure at any time.

I've always cherished the story of the pastor who preached verse by verse through the whole Bible. However when he finally reached the Book of Revelation, he simply read it to his people. As the reading finished they all jumped to their feet, raised their arms in the air and for half an hour there was a spontaneous outbreak of praise.

This is a healthy reminder that beyond a detailed analy- sis of this book we should be encouraged to worship, for the final victory of God is declared. It's been said that if you sneak a look at the last page of the Bible, what you find in Revelation is that God wins!

What kind of literature?

It is helpful to understand the kind of book that Revelation actually is when we are reading it. Firstly, it is written in an *apocalyptic* style, as are the books of Daniel and Zechariah, but there were also many non-biblical books of this type. This style of writing is characterised by being full of numbers and symbols. It is a kind of code language and the readers had to crack the code. It could be used to make political statements in an indirect way. John draws heavily on symbols already present in the Old Testament. It would be quite incorrect to visualise every statement that John makes as something that will literally happen. There may be a code that needs to be deci- phered.

The book is written during a vision. We read several times that John is being told what to write down (e.g. Rev 1:11 and 19:9). Rather than viewing this book as a worked-over reflection of a vision that John once had, he is writing as the vision unfolds and he is seeking to convey the feeling and spirit of what he sees. To use ordinary language and phrases would have been, to say the least, somewhat restrictive when you are seeing visions of God and glory. We are meant to *feel* this book at least as much as try to explain it in every detail.

Also, this book claims itself to be prophecy. 'Blessed are the ones who read the words of this prophecy' (Rev 1:3, see also 22:19). Like so many of the Old Testament prophets, Revelation has something to say to its own age, to every age, but can also have explicit reference to the future.

Structure

The central figure of the book is Jesus, and the dominating theme is the victory of God. As John writes, the Church is facing persecution and will have much suffering to pass through in future generations. But Jesus has triumphed through his Cross and resurrection and everything will be brought to a glorious conclusion at his return.

The first five chapters have some details that cause debate among scholars and commentators, but the overall structure is clear enough.

After a brief introduction John describes a wonderful vision of Christ and receives the commission to write down what he sees. The Letters to the seven churches are found in chapters 2 and 3. Some commentators would see in these letters seven ages of church history, with us inevitably living in the Laodicean age, which is marked by a spiritual lukewarmness. This could be considered as a very subjective viewpoint because we could theoretically be in any of the seven ages, since we do not know the date of Christ's return.

These seven letters were written to real churches in existence at the time and were expected to produce a response. If the glorified Christ sent a personal letter to our church I guess we would probably want to respond! From these letters there are lessons to learn, encouragements and warnings that remain relevant to every church at every point of church history, and will remain so until the end.

Moving on to chapters 4 and 5, John describes his vision of heaven, introduced with the words, 'After this I looked and there before me was a door standing open in heaven'. Before we look at the chaotic scenes on earth we are able to fix our eyes on heaven and the One who occupies the throne of the universe.

A scene of great beauty is described and we are given a picture of the Lamb – slain, but now risen. The redeemed, the angels and all creation praise God and the Lamb. The twenty-four Elders who are mentioned as part of the praising community almost certainly represent the whole people of God.

There is a search for someone who is worthy to break the seals and open a scroll. This scroll can be seen as a record of God's judgements and deliverances, which will take place to complete his purposes in the universe. The scroll is a symbol of the promise of the future kingdom. It has been documented and sealed up, but not yet carried out. By the sacrifice of Christ men have been purchased to reign on the earth. So the Lamb is the one worthy to open the seals and initiate God's judgements, which will be consummated in the glorious coming of the Kingdom.

Three series of sevens

These seals are the first of three series of sevens. Later we read of the seven trumpets and the seven bowls. These series of sevens remain the subject of much debate. I stand with those who see them referring to parallel events. G. R. Beasley-Murray writes:

> It appears to be beyond contradiction that an identical point of time is reached at the end of each series of judgements depicted under the symbols of the seven seals, seven trumpets and seven bowls, that point is the coming of the kingdom of God.[1]

It would be generally agreed that the three sevens do take us the climax of history, but Beasley-Murray makes an additional point: 'It is important that we should recognise John's procedure in his prophecies. He is not piling on agony after agony in a meaningless profusion of torments. He characterises the period of the last tribulation from a series of different viewpoints.'[2]

However, whereas G. R. Beasley-Murray sees these three series as parallel events in the time of the tribulation, it is possible to see them as parallel events that cover the whole of church history. It has often been pointed out that the seals of Revelation chapter 6 read very much like the signs of Mark chapter 13, so it is possible to argue that the whole of world history since the time of Christ has been full of war, international strife and persecution for the Church. The seals give us such a picture. The opening of the sixth seal describes the day which will end world history and bring us to the very brink of Christ's return, for it uses exactly the same kind of language that describes the events immediately before the return of Christ as we read it in the gospels (see Rev 6:12–17).

In chapter 7 we have an 'interlude' before the seventh seal is broken. Coming before the opening of the seventh seal what we appear to be reading here is about the security of the Church. The six seals have described world history until the return of Christ; but what of the status and situation of the Church during this period? Revelation chapter 7 tells us about this.

Who are the 144,000 who are sealed in verse 4? This suspiciously tidy number is surely a symbol and not a statistic. Some interesting mathematical formulae have been attempted to prove this number represents completeness. Although Israelite tribes are named as making up the number of 144,000, it would seem in context that we should understand this symbol as the whole Church of God. In verse 9, the 144,000 become a multitude too great to number, again indicating that the 144,000 is symbolic, referring to all God's redeemed people who are now seen standing before the throne.

The servants of God are sealed as a picture of their absolute security, so that no matter what tribulation or suffering they pass through, they will be kept safe forever, for the seal of God is upon them.

We then come to the opening of the seventh seal that ushers in the eternal age. There is a seventh seal, but John is not yet given further revelation about it.

As we move on to the events heralded by the seven trumpets we note again that these can be read as parallel to the events unfolded by the breaking of the seven seals. The seals can be understood as having particular reference to the sufferings of the Church during history and therefore the security of the Church needed emphasis. In chapter 8 the trumpets, covering the same span of history, proclaim a warning to an unbelieving world.

There is an 'interlude' between the sixth and seventh trumpets just as there was between the sixth and seventh seals. In this interlude we read of the ministry of the Church during world history. In John's own day the struggle in which Christians are involved is much more than the resistance of a little group to Caesar worship. Their struggle is part of a more terrifying contest in which Satan strives through politics and religion to thwart God's purposes for the Church. John shows us the role of the Church in midst of such pressures.

We are now at chapter 11 and half way through the book as John gives a rather complex picture of two witnesses. Other interpretations are possible but in the context of the Church's life at this point these two witnesses could well symbolise the ministry and mission of the Church. There will come a short time near the end (symbolically three-and-a-half days) when that mission seems to be over, for the two witnesses are put to death. But then the breath of God enters them and they live again, caught up to the glory of the living God while their enemies look on.

This is a difficult passage of Revelation but the main issue is clear: the vindication of God's saints and their triumph over the forces of evil represented in the Antichrist (of whom more is to be said) will be complete.

After this interlude we return again to the trumpets and the seventh one is sounded. As with the seventh seal we cannot doubt that with this trumpet blown we are again brought to the time of Christ's return.

The Church in conflict

Before we come to the last series of sevens – the seven bowls – John gives us a picture of the conflict between the Church and the evil powers in chapters 12–14. At the beginning of chapter 12 a reference to a son born of a woman whom Satan seeks to devour is one of the most controversial symbols in the whole book. Is the son to be understood as Christ or the Church? Personally, I believe it is possible to see Christ and the Church as intertwined here; after all, the Church is the Body of Christ. The saints are able to be overcomers because Christ by his atoning death and mighty resurrection defeated the devil's claim to man, and believers share his victory as they confess the testimony that is the gospel. The accuser has no room in heaven – he is thrown out and does his work on the earth.

Having been flung out of heaven, Satan, now represented as a dragon, stands on the seashore and calls out of the sea a Beast (the Antichrist) to help him. Another beast, usually referred to as the False Prophet, a master of signs and wonders, joins him. The Beast takes both political and religious power and the False Prophet forces people to worship him.

The reign of the Antichrist is limited to forty-two months and remains under the hand of God. Luther once said that the devil must be seen as God's devil. He can never step beyond the boundaries set by God, nor can he frustrate God's ultimate purpose.

This passage can be seen as marking both the spirit of Antichrist, which is always in the world, but also the evil that is finally concentrated in one man known as the Antichrist. This certainly fits in with the teaching in John's first letter concerning the Antichrist.

Finally in this section we see that there will only be torment for the followers of the Beast, but the saints who persevere will be blessed even in death.

We are turned to Christ's Parousia yet again as angels are sent forth to harvest the earth and God's wrath and judgement fall upon the nations.

As we read next of the seven bowls which are poured out it may be that we are meant to see here a picture of an intensification of God's judgement towards the end of history. This time there is no interlude; we go from bowl six immediately to bowl seven and the events that accompany Christ's return.

In chapters 17 and 18 we are shown what happens to the anti-Christian power at the close of the age. The mention of Babylon in these chapters seems to portray a corrupt commercial and political spirit. A woman is called 'Babylon the great'. The woman shows a nature like that of the city against which the prophets of former days spoke. She is a prostitute and being associated with Babylon indicates that any pleasure can be enjoyed as long as you come up with the money.

Undoubtedly the city of Rome is being referred to in terms of Babylon, especially with reference to its seven hills (Rev 17:9). John does what the prophets have often done; he sets the Day of the Lord in relation to his own day. The expectation is of a culmination of wickedness on the earth in a great resistance to Christ and his kingdom through the Antichrist and his realm. Rome, in John's day, was beginning to play the part of the Antichrist. As the Church was faced with a devastating persecution by Rome, so the Church of the last days will find itself opposed by worldly powers. But worldly structures will collapse. God's kingdom will be established as Christ returns.

There then comes the celebration of Babylon's downfall, the eternal ruin of the city of the Antichrist forming a vivid contrast to the eternal glory of the city of God.

One of the fascinating aspects of the whole passage is how the prostitute is somehow also the city (see Rev 17:18). Probably her prostitution is a personification of the evils of the city. Interestingly, the Church is also a woman and a city and we have already seen in an earlier chapter how in Revelation chapter 21 she is described as a City and a Bride. So, the Bride replaces the prostitute and Babylon is replaced by Jerusalem. Christ has his Woman and his City, which is the Church.

Hallelujah!

Events now take a definite upturn! The Wedding Supper of the Lamb is described in chapter 19, as the Church and Christ are joined in celebration forever. This clearly follows the Second Coming of Christ which is then described in the second half of this chapter, as Jesus Christ rides forth on a white horse, King of Kings and Lord of Lords.

The final chapters describe what happens following the Second Coming of Christ, events which we have recorded in earlier chapters. It's exactly at this point that some would argue that Revelation chapter 20 follows the description of Christ's return in chapter 19, and therefore must record his 1000-year reign on the earth: it cannot suddenly be read as a flashback that covers all of history up until the second coming of Christ. In other words this is an argument in favour of Pre-Millennialism and against A-Millennialism. However we have already seen that the three series of sevens may well keep taking us back to a complete overview of history rather than moving us forward in time with each new set of sevens. And even in chapter 19 we have already noted that the Wedding Supper of the Lamb is followed by a description of Christ's return, though chronologically it follows it. So there is no problem once we have accepted that Revelation contains a *number* of flashbacks to argue that the 1000 years of Revelation chapter 20 is also a flashback covering all of Christian history.

The last section of Revelation gives us the picture of final judgement and the new heavens and new earth. John has had the revelation: Our God reigns, forever and forever.

The last page of the last book of the Bible ends with the news that God wins.

Notes

1. G. R. Beasley-Murray, *Highlights of the Book of Revelation*, Broadman Press, 1972, p. 46.
2. Ibid., p. 48.

10

Israel

Many Christians feel passionately about the nation of Israel. We must take care that emotion does not over-ride good biblical exegesis. Clearly God had an original plan for Israel, but the nation failed to fulfil it because of her disobedience. However God still determines to have a people who will fulfil his purpose. Romans 9–11 however seems to make very clear that God still has an end-time plan for the nation of Israel. We must also look at the very controversial areas raised by Israel's present status, particularly the basis of her claim to the land, whether the nation or the Church today is fulfilling Old Testament prophecies and whom exactly does the Bible regard now as the People of God.

Israel

No book taking a broad view of the end times can over-look the subject of Israel. It is here that any writer is likely to lose some friends and gain others! All evangelical Christians claim to base their views on the Bible. I am making my own attempt to be thoroughly biblical on this issue. Not every reader will agree with all my views, but I hope all will understand my desire to handle this contro-versial area with integrity.

Original purpose

We will begin with a point that is not really in dispute and therefore can be looked at briefly, and that is God's origi-nal purpose for Israel. God called a pagan called Abraham who believed God, having been chosen by him to be the Father of the Jewish nation. God's relationship with Abraham and the nation was one of covenant. God promised to be their God and the strength of that rela-tionship is seen in the often repeated phrase, 'the God of Abraham, Isaac and Jacob'.

Israel, as God's nation, was to live obediently before him, especially in the single-mindedness of her worship and devotion. Jehovah is the one true God and Israel his people. But there was a purpose in his choice of this nation, that she should be a witness to him as the one true God. 'You are my witnesses, declares the Lord, that I am God' (Isa 43:12). Israel would be in a unique position to demonstrate the blessings to be derived from belonging to God, 'Blessed are the people whose God is the Lord' (Ps 144:15).

So often the history of Israel was far from one of faithfulness to God and his purpose for her; rather it was one of apostasy and spiritual prostitution. As a result Israel was punished for her sin. Destruction fell on the nation at the hands of the Assyrians and the Babylonians. Jews were taken into exile in the North, though later to return in a time of restoration to their own nation. Beyond this, all we need to note here is that according to the New Testament God has persisted in his desire to have his own nation of people who might live with purpose to their lives. 'Jesus Christ, who gave himself for us to redeem us from all wickedness and to purify for himself a people that are his very own, eager to do what is good' (Titus 2:14).

Israel and the end times

But does God have a particular purpose at the end of the age for Israel? We need to refer to Romans 9–11, which are not easy chapters as they deal with the subject of election – a subject which strains our emotions as well as our intellect.

Right through these chapters there are several references to Israel. On each occasion it is clear that Paul is speaking about the Jewish nation. He speaks of his passionate desire to see his own race, the people of Israel, saved. He argues that as in the time of Elijah there was a remnant of righteous people in the nation, so even now there is from that nation a remnant chosen by grace. Indeed he makes clear that God still has a continuing interest in the nation. Certainly Israel's fall has given the opportunity for the gospel to reach the Gentiles, but they should not be arrogant lest judgement fall on them.

Now we need to give particular attention to two verses near the end of Romans chapter 11. 'I do not want you to be ignorant of this mystery, brothers, so that you may not be conceited: Israel has experienced a hardening in part until the full number of Gentiles has come in. And so all Israel will be saved . . .'(v. 25, 26).

The phrase 'And so all Israel will be saved' has been taken by some to refer to the Church, all God's elect, converted Jew and Gentile. It's simply saying that finally all God's people are gathered in and saved. The problem with this interpretation is that it makes the word 'Israel' mean something different to every other occasion on which it has been used in these chapters. Indeed even in the previous sentence (quoted above) the term Israel clearly means the Jewish race as the contrast is made with Gentiles. To suggest that suddenly the word 'Israel' now means something else, that is, the Church, is surely to claim that in the Bible words only mean what I want them to mean at the time.

The expression 'all Israel' was used by the rabbis to describe the nation as a whole, not to refer to literally every individual Jew. So to say, 'all Israel will be saved' is to indicate a major turning of the nation to God. Iain Murray writes: 'This is not to say that every individual

Israelite will be converted: despite the thousands of believing Jews in the Apostolic period, the casting away of the Jews was so general that it permitted the assertion that Israel was cast off, so, despite those who will remain unbelieving, the number to be ingathered will be of an extent which justifies the expression "all Israel will be saved."'[1]

This ingathering of Israel needs to be recognised as a truly end-time event. As Eldon Ladd points out, 'Whatever the means of Israel's salvation it appears to be an eschatological event in Paul's thought. It is impossible that Israel should be saved in any way but by faith in Jesus in her Messiah.'[2]

How are we to understand this turning of the nation to Jesus and her salvation? It could happen as an accelerating work of conversion occurs among the Jews as the full number of Gentiles is coming to completion (Romans 11:25).

Or should we understand it as a literal end-time event? We read in Revelation 1:7 that when Christ returns every eye will see him. Could it be that at the first glimpse of the returning Christ, Israel turns and calls on him as her Messiah?

Some object to the possibility of this second interpretation on the basis of a statement in chapter 11. 'But if their transgression means riches for the world, and their loss means riches for the Gentiles, how much greater riches will their fullness bring!' (v. 12). It is suggested that this implies that the world generally will have time to enjoy great blessings because of Israel's conversion. But it could simply be understood as an expression of wonder that the Jewish nation will yet experience salvation.

The precise details of Israel's conversion as a nation cannot be fixed from scripture, but what is clear is that

God has an end time purpose for the nation. Israel will believe on Jesus and 'all Israel will be saved'.

Israel and the present time

Now to the most controversial area of all, which is Israel's present status and position. On this, Christians are widely divided. To put the opposite positions: some would claim that Israel is no more, or less, significant than any other nation. Israel is one nation on the earth from which believers will come just as they will come from every other nation. Beyond that there is nothing more to say. At the other extreme are those who hold what is called a Dispensational view. God's real purposes are focused on Israel; the Church is just an interlude in what God is seeking to do finally with his nation, the Jews.

The task of the Church must always be seeking to establish the true biblical position. So what is Israel's present status? We will look at three separate areas.

The land

On the 14th May 1948 David Ben Gurion read a Declaration of Independence announcing the establishment of the Jewish nation to be known as the state of Israel. Was this a fulfilment of prophecy? Bruce Milne writes:

Many passages predicting the restoration of the Jews appear to refer to the immediate historical context in the Old Testament, that is, their return from exile in Babylon (Deut 30:1–10; Ezek 36:17–24; Hos 11:10f). These promises are made to a remnant of the whole nation who had faith in the Lord, a condition certainly not met in the events of this century, but met in those who returned from Babylon . . . on the other hand, some of the Old Testament prophecies appear, on the surface at least, to cover more than a restoration from Babylon (Jer 29:4; Ezek 38:24–28; Amos 9:15; Zec 8:1–8) . . . Equating biblical references to Israel with the present secularised state of Israel appears distinctly questionable.[3]

This seems to leave all the options open, but at least it causes us to recognise that all prophecies of Israel's restoration to the land cannot simply and easily be said to have been totally fulfilled by the return from exile in Babylon hundreds of years before Christ. It has been claimed that perhaps one in eight of the Old Testament's prophecies of Israel's return to the land cannot refer to the return from Babylon. Here is an example. 'I will plant Israel in their own land, never again to be uprooted from the land I have given them, says the Lord your God' (Amos 9:15). It is impossible to claim that the promise here was fulfilled in the return from exile because the Romans uprooted Israel from her land again.

So there are two ways of regarding Israel's present undeniable occupation of the land. It is either a fulfilment of prophecies going back thousands of years or a combination of luck, political manoeuvring and military success. However, in the end, the matter is undeniably centred on the issue of covenant.

In Genesis chapter 17, verses 7 and 8, God makes a covenant promise to Abraham. He will be with Abraham and the generations that will succeed him. It is specifically referred to as an everlasting covenant and the land is promised to Abraham and his descendants as an everlasting possession. This could be regarded as settling the issue. God has made an everlasting covenant and included in that there is the promise of the land forever. But that is challenged by the very next verse, 'Then God said to Abraham, "As for you, you must keep my covenant, you and your descendants after you for the generations to come"' (Gen 17:9). So the argument is sometimes made that the generation that followed Abraham broke covenant and therefore forfeited the promised blessings including the possession of the land as an absolute right. However, this promise will find a spiritual fulfilment in the Church.

The crux of the issue is this: was God's covenant with Israel conditional or unconditional? If it was unconditional then the covenant promises belong to national Israel whether in faith or sin. If the conditions are faith and obedience, however, then the promises belong to those who have the same faith as Abraham, that is, the Church. David Mansell writes:

> What about the many scriptures stating that the land was to be an everlasting possession? For example, 'the whole land of Canaan, where you are now an alien, I will give as an everlasting possession to you and your descendants after you: and I will be their God. (Gen 17:18)

> The land was part of God's covenant promise to Abraham, yet God had told Abraham, 'As for you, you must keep my covenant'. (Gen 17:19)

> So what about the promise of eternal possession? Has God's promise failed? Of course not. The problem only arises when we confuse the natural with the spiritual.

> The promise of eternal possession guarantees the world to believers in Jesus, not the land to ethnic Israel. Those who

are of the faith of Abraham are the heirs, not just of the land
of Israel, but of the world. (Rom 4:13)

Unbelieving Israel, then, has no biblical ground upon which
it can establish a divine title to the land. It does, however,
have an historical claim along with the 'aliens' or 'strangers'
who lived alongside it.[4]

In his paper *The Church and Israel*, David Blomgren
writes: 'The emphasis of the connection of the grafted
Gentile branches with the root of which they partake
shows that the church being grafted in becomes all that
national Israel was in the OT. The church not only
receives the blessings of Israel, but by being grafted in the
church *becomes* the Israel of God to the extent that unbelieving national Israel no longer is.'[5]

These two writers appear to be coming from the same
theological base: the Church has replaced Israel and
receives all her promises. But David Blomgren also writes,
'The gift of land to Abraham and his physical descendants which they had formerly possessed is irrevocable by
God because it was eternal and unconditional. The New
Testament writers do not disinherit national Israel from
the land because it is an everlasting possession (Gen
17:8)'.[6] So, although these two writers agree on the
Church replacing Israel, they disagree on the issue of the
land, because they disagree over the issue of covenant.

I would argue that there is an unconditional covenant
with Israel on this issue. It is true that Israel was charged
with keeping the covenant, but she is not told that she will
forfeit the land if she fails to do so. Indeed God always
promises to bring Israel back (see Lev 26:42–45).
Abraham is charged, at this time, with keeping the

covenant through the practice and mark of circumcision. In context, it is the breaking of the covenant when the male is not circumcised that will cause him to be cut off from the people of God (Gen 17:10–14). T. E. McComiskey puts this issue clearly:

> The promise of the land is an eternal promise, yet the NT seems to contain not one unequivocal affirmation that the promise of the land will be fulfilled for the Jewish people within the definable boundaries of Palestine. In fact the NT expands that promise to include the whole world (Rom 4:13) . . . But what of the literal restoration of the land to Israel? The answer may be found in part in a principle that is emerging from this study (of covenant theology). That is, the promise undergoes expansion but it never suffers observable abrogation . . . if the NT does not emphasise a literal restoration of Israel to the land it may be because the Gentile church is largely in view. It is at best arguing from silence to deny a continuing promise of land for Israel because of a lack of emphasis in the NT.[7]

I would maintain that Israel's present possession of the land is not only because of a legal declaration by the United Nations but by extraordinary (surely miraculous) military preservation. I believe God's fingerprints are seen all over this. The covenant promise is being fulfilled.

Israel's occupation of the land says nothing, necessarily, about the present spiritual state of the nation. Israel does not have any moral right to treat unjustly those now found within her borders as aliens. She is surely entitled to defend herself from attack and aggression both within and from without her borders. But if those who are unregenerate and even atheist govern the nation, we must not be surprised if there are some violations of human rights.

To criticise Israel's present politics is not to be anti-Semitic, but to be hostile to Israel's very existence and every action, clearly is.

Some raise the question of the purpose or meaning of Israel's present return to the land. I offer the following suggestions:

a. It is a testimony to the faithfulness of a God who keeps covenant. 'He remembers his covenant forever, the word he commanded, for a thousand generations, the covenant he swore to Isaac. He confirmed it to Jacob as a decree, to Israel as an everlasting covenant: To you I will give the land of Canaan as the portion you will inherit' (Ps 105:8–11).
b. It is a sign, that as God is fulfilling his promise to Israel, he will fulfill his promises to the Church.
c. The land of Israel and indeed the city of Jerusalem are physical, earthly signs that always point to a greater fulfilment. Those who are the heirs of Abraham in that they have faith, like Abraham, do not now simply possess a narrow strip of physical land, but are destined to inherit the whole earth. 'It was not through law that Abraham and his offspring received the promise that he would be heir of the world, but through the righteousness that comes by faith.' (Rom. 4.13) Certainly as the Church penetrates every nation there is a working out of this, but there is still a final fulfilment to come when the Church shall inhabit a new earth. So the promise undergoes expansion for the Church.
d. It is a precursor to a national turning of Israel to Jesus in repentance and faith.

There are those who believe that all the promises about the land given to Israel are now transferred to the Church. That is not this writer's position, but to take such a view does not mean that a person is anti-Semitic or even anti-Israel as a nation. It has to be a matter of biblical conviction.

The nature of prophecy

Certain prophecies in the Old Testament have been interpreted in two very different ways. There are those who say that the prophecies are only for the nation of Israel, whereas others say they are now all transferred to the Church. Bible commentators will however often speak of prophetic scriptures that have an immediate fulfilment and also a future fulfilment.

In the so-called 'Restoration' chapters, such as Isaiah chapter 62, there is certainly an address to the situation of Israel in exile, but is there more than that? Surely whenever the People of God (and since Pentecost that is the Church, as we'll see below) get into a low state, then Isaiah chapter 62, and other similar chapters, are a reminder that there is always a hope of restoration for God's people and his work.

Sometimes the Holy Spirit 'highlights' particular scriptures to the Church. A notable example of this was the revelation that came to Martin Luther on justification by faith. This was not something new in scripture, but Luther suddenly 'saw it'. The history of the Church has been changed by what he saw.

Therefore one can argue that the Holy Spirit has 'highlighted' scriptures like Isaiah chapter 62 to the Church, and that this has led many to seek a restoration of the Church in our generation. Of course there may yet be other generations of Christians who will see a more thorough restoration of the Church than we are seeing in our day. Those who believe in Reconstructionism are certain this will happen.

Here are some helpful questions to put to prophetic scriptures:

a. Did this have an immediate, obvious fulfilment?
b. Can this only be related to ethnic Israel because of God's covenant promise?
c. Is there something in this prophecy that makes it relevant for all generations of God's people?
d. Is there an interpretation of this prophecy given in the New Testament?

The primary importance of the Church

Scripture is its own interpreter. So we find that there are certain passages in the Old Testament which are clearly interpreted in the New Testament with reference to the Church. This touches on the issue of what we can call the 'true Israel'.

> For not all who are descended from Israel are Israel. Nor because they are his descendants are they all Abraham's children. On the contrary, "It is through Isaac that your offspring will be reckoned." In other words, it is not the natural children who are God's children, but it is the children of the promise who are regarded as Abraham's offspring. (Rom 9:6–8)

Clearly we are being told in the New Testament that we cannot regard all the natural descendants of Abraham as the true Israel. Who then are the true Israel? In the quote just given, Paul says, 'it is the children of the promise who are regarded as Abraham's offspring'. This is such a telling point that it is repeated elsewhere in Romans.

> A man is not a Jew if he is only one outwardly, nor is circumcision merely outward and physical. No, a man is a Jew if he is one inwardly; and circumcision is circumcision of the heart . . . (Rom 2:28–29)
>
> . . . we have been saying that Abraham's faith was credited to him as righteousness. Under what circumstances was it credited? Was it after he was circumcised or before? It was not after, but before! And he received the sign of circumcision, a seal of the righteousness that he had by faith while he was still circumcised. So then, he is the father of all who believe but have not been circumcised, in order that righteousness might be credited to them. And he is also the father of the circumcised who not only are circumcised but who also walk in the footsteps of the faith that our father Abraham had before he was circumcised. (Rom 4:9–12)

Using the terms the New Testament uses, the descendants of Abraham, the children of God, the true Israel *are those of like faith with Abraham*. They could be Jew or Gentile. The essential and qualifying point is that like Abraham they believe God and are therefore declared righteous. 'If you belong to Christ, then you are Abraham's seed, and heirs according to the promise' (Gal 3:29).

All this is further underlined by the fact that there are terms used of Israel in the Old Testament that are clearly transferred to the Church in the New Testament: 'chosen people', 'a royal priesthood', 'a holy nation', 'a people belonging to God' (see 1 Peter 2:9).

So, now, the Church – comprising believing Jews and Gentiles – must be regarded as the children of God, the

People of God, and not ethnic Israel. 'The Greek word "ekklesia" is the word most commonly used in the Greek OT to refer to Israel as the People of God. The very use of the words suggest that our Lord purposed to bring into existence a new people who would take the place of the old Israel who rejected both His claim to Messiahship and His offer of the Kingdom of God.'[8]

In other words, although I believe that there is an end-time purpose for ethnic Israel in terms of the salvation of the nation as a whole, and although I believe we are seeing covenant promises fulfilled in Israel's possession of the land, I would maintain that it is absolutely and abundantly clear that only the Church comprising believers, both Jew and Gentile, can now be referred to as the People of God. Alan Vincent writes:

> We are told that they (the Jews) will be provoked to jealousy when they see God's blessing upon the Gentiles and that this will convict them and cause them to be saved. So it seems to me that the greatest practical thing we can do to bring Jews to Christ is to make the church so magnificent and so glorious, so evidently blessed of God and so rich in all the promises which God made to Abraham, that the Jews are forced to take notice and be provoked to seek this God themselves, so that they might be saved.[9]

Conclusion

What conclusions can we draw from all this? I suggest the following.

1. Let us recognise and be thankful that our Saviour comes from Jewish descent after the flesh.

2. Scripture encourages us to pray for the peace of Jerusalem. We should not ignore that. World peace is largely dependent on the peace of Jerusalem. It is also surely a reminder to pray for other troubled parts of the world.

3. I believe we should defend Israel's right to be in the land. She has been granted land legally by agreement of the world's nations. She has an historical claim. It is a fulfilment of God's covenant promises.

4. We should not defend Israel's politics if they are unjust or oppressive to those caught up within her borders. Indeed the Old Testament teaches the right treatment of those who are aliens in the land.

5. Keep a close eye on Israel because the Jewish people have a part within the end-time purposes of God.

6. We should recognise that some within a local church may have an evangelistic and/or prayer burden for Israel that is as legitimate as others may have for, say, China. We have no need to squash that, nor is there any need to make it the burden of the whole Church. However, if the nation of Israel will finally turn to Christ we should not regard that fatalistically, but consider what part we could take to speed that process.

7. In some cities or towns there may be a definite Jewish community. This could be considered as worthy of special attention in the same way as an Indian or student community may be so considered in another town.

8. Resist the view that God has finished with the nation of Israel, but also resist the view that Israel must be the central focus of church life.

Our understanding of the end times will affect the way we build the Church. If we have a concern for the Jews the best way to reach them is to build a glorious Church – to provoke them to envy and to hasten the coming in of the full number of the Gentiles.

And so all Israel will be saved.

Notes

1.   Iain Murray, *The Puritan Hope*, Banner of Truth, 1975, p. 68.
2.   Eldon Ladd, G., *A Theology of the New Testament*, Lutterworth, 1994.
3.   Bruce Milne, *Know the Truth*, IVP, 1982, 1984, pp. 261–2.
4.   David Mansell, 'Israel and God's Word: Abraham and the Land' *Restoration Magazine*. 6/1982, p. 32.
5.   David Blomgren, *The Church and Israel*, Unpublished paper, undated, p. 94.
6.   Ibid., p. 136.
7.   Thomas E. McComiskey, *The Covenants of Promise: A Theology of Old Testament Covenants*, IVP, 1985.
8.   Eldon Ladd, *op. cit.*
9.   Alan Vincent, *Jews and Gentiles – God's End-Time Purposes*, paper delivered to elders training in Woking.

11

A Demonstrating Church

Our eschatology should affect our ecclesiology. Or to put it in rather simpler theological terminology, the way we view the end times should affect the way we are building the local church right now. When you believe the Rapture will take place and what you believe about the condition of the Church when Jesus returns will certainly influence your view of the Church today and the task to be done. God's desire according to Ephesians is that the Church should right now demonstrate the multicoloured wisdom of God. We are observed in the Church by cosmic powers. Our churches can be built to thrill angels and frighten demons.

A Demonstrating Church

I am convinced that what we believe about the end times will affect the way we build the local church. In these final chapters I will work this out in the light of the eschatological convictions expressed in this book.

It has sometimes been jokingly suggested that if we really believe in the Pre-Tribulation Rapture of the Church we should drive soft-topped cars. This presumably would save us from brain damage if the unexpected and sudden rapture of Christians took place while we were driving along the M25!

I once had a friend who visited the USA who, when he came home, reported that he had met a man selling Tribulation fruit. This believer was clearly convinced that the Church would pass through the Tribulation and now was the opportunity to store cans of tinned fruit so that in the age of the Antichrist there would be a food resource.

Either of these actions would suggest that Christians were allowing their eschatology to affect the way they plan and live. On a broader perspective our eschatological viewpoint must affect the way we build the local church right now.

A key verse on building the Church is to be found in Paul's letter to Ephesus: 'His (God's) intent was that now, through the church, the manifold wisdom of God should be made known to the rulers and authorities in the heavenly realms' (Eph 3:10). We assume that when God says 'now' it means that the Church is to demonstrate the wisdom of God in the present time.

What does the text mean when it refers to God's 'manifold wisdom'? The Greek word translated 'manifold' is *polupoikilos*, which means a great variety of colour. In the Greek translation of the Old Testament, Joseph's coat is described as *poikilos*, that is, many-coloured, but the wisdom of God is *polupoikilos* – an even stronger term. The variety and colour of God's wisdom is seen both in creation and in history, but its central focus is undoubtedly the person of Christ. Paul writes, 'Jews demand miraculous signs and Greeks look for wisdom, but we preach Christ crucified: a stumbling block to Jews and foolishness to Gentiles, but to those whom God has called, both Jews and Greeks, Christ is the power of God and the wisdom of God' (1 Cor 1:22–24).

So here we see that Christ is described as the wisdom of God, but a few verses later on there is an explanation of why Christ can be understood like that: 'It is because of him that you are in Christ Jesus, who has become for us wisdom from God – that is, our righteousness, holiness and redemption' (1 Cor 1:30). God's wisdom is seen in that while we were cut off from God in an utterly helpless condition because of our sin, God knew what to do. Christ was the answer to our sin and separation and therefore he is the wisdom of God for us. Through Christ we are declared righteous; through him we are being made holy; and by him we have been redeemed. His blood was the price paid to ransom us from slavery to sin. This manifold wisdom of God, which is Jesus Christ and the difference he makes, needs to be made known.

If God's wisdom is to be demonstrated, who is it that he wants to know about it? We might think the answer must be the peoples of the world. Certainly in verse 9 Paul speaks of making the gospel plain to everyone. But Paul's emphasis in verse 10 is that God's wisdom should be demonstrated to the rulers and the authorities in the heavenly realms. Who are these rulers and authorities? There are two credible answers: angels or demons.

The case for the *angels* is this. Jesus lives in heavenly realms according to Ephesians 2:6. Where Jesus is there are surely angels. Also we know that the angels have a particular interest in the Church, not only stooping down to look into the things that pertain to salvation according to Peter (1 Peter 1:12), but apparently also observing the Church. In 1 Corinthians 11 the Church is encouraged by Paul to maintain a godly order 'because of the angels' (1 Cor 11:10).

So if the angels inhabit heavenly realms and through countless ages have been observing the wisdom of God in his acts of creation and interventions in history, then there is also something else for them to watch. They see that from all the nations a people are coming together as the Church, and they are agog with the wonder of it.

There is also an argument for the *demons*. Ephesians 6:12 also talks about rulers and authorities in the heavenly realms, but the reference is clearly and unambiguously to demons. So maybe it is to the demons that the wisdom of God should be made known.

Of course it is possible that the reference is to both angels and demons. In general terms we can say that God's intention is that his wisdom should be demonstrated to cosmic powers.

Some are bound to ask the question, why? We can only make suggestions here. Certainly we know that the angels rejoice over repentant sinners and according to the writer to the Hebrews there are myriads of them in joyful assembly. The angels of God are sinless and cannot be redeemed, but they are thrilled to see sinners redeemed. So making known the manifold wisdom of God is likely to excite and enthral angelic beings.

The demons need reminding that they are on the losing side. To declare God's wisdom to them, which is Christ, will force demonic forces to retreat.

We need next to ask the question, how is God's manifold wisdom to be demonstrated to the cosmic powers? The answer is, through the Church. Commenting on this scripture, Dr Martyn Lloyd Jones says, 'In other words we are given here a portrayal of the Church in her dignity and greatness and glory which, in a sense, really seems to surpass anything the Apostle has ever said about her.'[1]

How do angels and demons see the demonstration of God's wisdom? What will cause angels to celebrate and demons to flee? Incredibly, but gloriously, it is the Church.

It is here we can understand that if we are not expecting an any-moment rapture of the Church, there really is still time to build demonstrating churches. Now is the time to build such churches, not expecting that we might simply be caught away at any moment or that we shall effortlessly flow into a golden age of gospel success. It is not a time either for hanging on nervously, simply preserving a remnant people in small congregations or even just holding on to our present gains in expectation that we may disappear skywards at any moment. This is the time, right now, to put on a demonstration of God's wisdom and to build the Church.

Let's see in practical terms how this can actually happen.

By declaration

Here in Ephesians chapter 3 Paul speaks of preaching the unsearchable, or infinite, riches of Christ (v. 8). A church that thrills the angels and terrifies the demons will be a church of declaration.

There is a place for corporate declaration. The words of the Nicene Creed, for example, proclaimed confidently and in faith by a local church, speak powerfully of the wisdom of God.

> I believe in one God the Father Almighty; Maker of heaven and earth, and of all things visible and invisible.
>
> And in one Lord Jesus Christ, the only-begotten Son of God, begotten of the Father before all worlds, God of God, Light of Light, very God of very God, begotten, not made, being of one substance with the Father; by whom all things were made; who, for us men and for our salvation, came down from heaven, and was incarnate by the Holy Spirit of the Virgin Mary, and was made man; and was crucified also for us under Pontius Pilate; he suffered and was buried; and the third day he rose again, according to the Scriptures; and ascended into heaven, and sitteth on the right hand of the Father; and he shall come again, with glory, to judge both the quick and the dead; whose kingdom shall have no end.

And in the Holy Spirit, the Lord and Giver of Life; who proceedeth from the Father and the Son; who with the Father and the Son together is worshipped and glorified; who spake by the Prophets. And one Holy Catholic and Apostolic Church. I acknowledge one Baptism for the remission of sins; and I look for the resurrection of the dead, and the life of the world to come. Amen.

That's a declaration to shake up the demons.

The wisdom of God is also declared by preaching. The truth proclaimed and accepted changes people's lives. If cosmic powers see people transformed by the declaration of God's wisdom then angels will rejoice and demons flee.

We declare:

> Christ has died.
> Christ has risen.
> Christ will come again.

By prayer

Again, in Ephesians chapter 3 we are reminded that in Christ we can freely and confidently approach God (v. 12). So through Jesus Christ, who is the wisdom of God, a people who once had no access to God, or if they thought they did had to do so through priestly mediation, are now free to approach him who is King of Kings and Lord of Lords. This is the incredible difference the wisdom of God makes to us.

There is no way that I could travel to London, enter Buckingham Palace and expect an immediate audience with the Queen expecting her to listen and answer my requests – even if I could prove my great loyalty as a

British citizen. Yet we can enter immediately and freely into the presence of the eternal and sovereign Lord and confidently ask him to grant our requests. Imagine the angels looking on; they are amazed. As for the demons, they are horrified, for this is the difference Christ has made to us.

By faith

Also in Ephesians 3:12 there is mention of our ability to approach God through faith in Christ. Faith must be present in authentic prayer, but faith can be identified as another element in a people transformed by the wisdom of God.

Here is something to thrill angels and depress demons, that there is a people who without sight will go to the edge and even over the edge because they believe God. The reality of the manifold wisdom of God is the difference Christ has made to people.

I am a pastor in a church which has undertaken an enormous church building project of over three and a half million pounds, by faith. There have been battles over building regulations, battles over permission to change a warehouse into a place of worship, battles because of bankrupt building firms who walked off site, and battles over finance. But the battles have been won by a people of faith whose trust in God is now tangibly seen in a modern church building and conference centre seating well over 1000 people. Christ changed us into risk-takers. Angels love it, demons hate it.

By unity

In Revelation 7:9–10 we read, 'After this I looked and there before me was a great multitude that no one could count, from every nation, tribe, people and language, standing before the throne and in front of the Lamb. They were wearing white robes and were holding palm branches in their hands. And they cried out in a loud voice: "Salvation belongs to our God, who sits on the throne, and to the Lamb."'

This description of the Church in glory must surely have some reflection in the Church on earth. These are not two entirely different species. The Church militant should demonstrate, if only as a pale reflection, the same marks as the Church triumphant.

The Church in glory is united. It is described as a people drawn together from every nation, tribe, people and language standing before the throne. What creates this unity? Certainly not the United Nations or the European Community. Rather it comes about through Jesus Christ who with his blood paid the price to purchase a people brought together, forever, as his Church.

As cosmic powers view our world, they will see its many divisions. What they should be able to see in the local church is a people who might not normally be expected to form any relationship but who have come together as a united community and are loving one another. Our local church has the capacity to amaze the angels and horrify the demons because we demonstrate a unity created by the wisdom of God.

By worship

The Church in heaven is full of worship. In the earlier quotation from Revelation we see the cry going up, 'Salvation belongs to our God, who sits on the throne.' Again and again in Revelation we read of a worshipping Church in heaven.

I've camped with thousands of other Christians at many Bible Weeks – a very down to earth experience! Emerging from tents and caravans, sometimes in pouring rain and sometimes in stifling heat, I've joined with these thousands in singing, clapping, dancing and shouting before God. Such a worshipping community in such conditions is a visible evidence of a people changed by the wisdom of God.

Every local church whose priority is that the living God be worshipped with great passion is able to enthral the angels and scare the demons. Again, we demonstrate the wisdom of God.

By growth

The Church in heaven, according to Revelation, is too vast in numbers to count. The angels must be thrilled to know they are not alone in their worship, but are joined by an immense company of the redeemed.

Would angels and demons see in the longings of your church a desire for immense growth in numbers? The Church in heaven will be huge, so why shouldn't we have some very big local churches on earth? If our attitude is 'I don't like it big' then perhaps we need to remember the angels and the demons. Angels would be overjoyed to see thousands in a town or city transformed by the wisdom of God. Surely demonic powers will tremble to see such a thing. In the longings of a local church there should be a desire for growth that will demonstrate God's wisdom to the cosmic powers.

A demonstrating Church is God's intention right now. If we are simply taken up with teaching about an any-moment rapture we may fail to build the local church now as God intends. There is time, but the time is now when the Church must set aside both small mindedness and an unhelpful eschatology to build a mighty demonstration of God's wisdom. Let the angels see it and rejoice; let the demons view it and flee.

Notes

1.   Martyn Lloyd Jones, *The Unsearchable Riches of Christ*, Banner of Truth, 1979, p. 81.

12

The Big Vision

Before Jesus comes again every people group will hear the gospel of Christ. Our view of how and when this will take place will be affected by our eschatology. The idea that such a task will be completed during the Tribulation period when the Church has been raptured is likely to make us more casual towards world mission. In fact we need a Big Vision *now* to reach all the peoples of the world. There is ground for confidence that such a vision will lead to success, but there also need to be strategies to implement the vision.

The Big Vision

If our understanding of the last things is going to affect the way we build the local church then we must accept the challenge of world mission.

The clearest statement that the Bible makes about the time of the end comes in Matthew 24:14: 'And this gospel of the kingdom will be preached in the whole world as a testimony to all nations, and then the end will come.' The Greek word translated as 'nations' means 'people groups' and this is surely how we are to understand it. To refer to a 'nation' as we use the word today is fairly meaningless in terms of this scripture. Nations change shape over the centuries. In Victorian times the nations of Africa were sometimes determined by colonial powers – which used a ruler and a pencil to draw national boundaries. But each separate people group, of whom there may be many within what today we call a nation, will hear the gospel and have a church. When this has happened, Jesus will return.

In Revelation 7:9 we read, 'After this I looked and there before me was a great multitude that no one could count, from every nation, tribe, people and language standing before the throne and in front of the Lamb . . .' John is seeing a vision of what takes place at the end of human history. What he sees is that every people group is represented among God's redeemed people before the throne.

If every people group will have a church before Jesus comes again – and that is his promise – and if John has seen that it happens, we must conclude that it has not yet happened and there is work to do.

Many argue the case for much more church planting to take place in the United Kingdom. Our present number of church buildings would only accommodate 16 per cent of the population if they were full, and the situation is usually worse in our bigger cities. However we need to consider that, even with the number of churches already established, there are surely enough to get the message of the gospel heard throughout this nation. Isn't it therefore right that the priority in mission and church planting should become the unreached people groups of the world? Our eschatology needs to affect our outlook on this subject. If I believe that the Church will not be raptured, and that Jesus will not return until there is a church in every people group, then each local church must be built with the big vision of the world's nations in its view.

A notable expansion in church mission came when the Apostle Paul, in debate with some jealous and abusive Jews, quoted from Isaiah: 'I have made you a light for the Gentiles, that you may bring salvation to the ends of the earth.' Paul saw this as a command from the Word to take the gospel of the Kingdom to the Gentile nations. We cannot rest content simply to see our hometown reached with the gospel. We must have the big vision; certainly, there is our county and nation to consider, but beyond that are the nations among whom are many people groups as yet ignorant of the gospel of the Kingdom who must have a church before Jesus comes again.

If as Pastors or Elders of our local churches our concern is only for the churches we lead, then our vision is too small. If as home group leaders our vision is only for the groups of 10 or 12 people we oversee, then the vision is too small. If as the treasurer of my local church my vision is simply to keep the accounts for this one church in the black, then the vision is way too small. Our sights must be set on the distant horizon. I am overseeing the money for a local church that must release resources to world mission. I am overseeing this small group of people that they might have the nations in their heart. I am Pastor of this local church, which exists in major part to pray for the nations, to send teams out on mission and to see resources of people and finance released to the establishment of churches in as yet unreached people groups of the world. We must have the big vision, for the task has to be completed before Jesus comes again. Robert Warren writes:

> We long for growth to take off. We look at our churches and say, 'Lord what do you need us to become?' These two words are part of the answer: a missionary congregation. When you see it, it's so obvious. Much of the Church of England's way of working derives from 400 years ago when most people were regular members. No-one setting up a church today would saddle it with the structures, buildings and hierarchies which we have inherited. And that's the point, in a Christian age we needed a pastoral church. In the largely pagan age of today, we need a missionary church and that is profoundly different. What does a missionary congregation look like? No-one knows. Are there any in Britain? Possibly not. A

missionary congregation is not a pastoral one with evangelistic activities bolted on. It is more radical than that.[1]

Robert Warren also writes: 'At the heart of the distinction
that is being made in this paper between a pastoral and
missionary church, is the difference between a church
organised around sustaining and developing and promoting its own life, and a church organised around par-
ticipating in God's mission in the world.'[2]

Exaggeration!

It is interesting to see how in the New Testament we often
read verses that seem to exaggerate when they speak of
the nations! Here are a few examples.

In Romans 15:19 Paul writes: '. . . So from Jerusalem
all the way round to Illyricum, I have fully proclaimed the
gospel of Christ' (Rom 15:19). Illyricum is modern
Yugoslavia. Can Paul really claim to have fully preached
the gospel over such a huge section of the Roman Empire
with no modern technology or modern transportation
available to him? Has he preached the gospel to every
person in such a vast area! It sounds like an exaggeration.
What he probably means is that, as he has proclaimed
Christ and planted churches, he only moved on when a
church was strong enough to maintain itself *and* had the
resources to evangelise its own people group. It is through
the planting of local churches with the motivation to
reach others in their own language and culture that every
community is going to be penetrated with the gospel.

In Colossians 1:6 we read, '. . . All over the world this
gospel is bearing fruit and growing, just as it has been
among you since the day you heard it and understood

God's grace in all its truth.' Paul clearly has the nations in his heart. Whatever Paul understood as the world in his day, today it is certainly true that the gospel is bearing fruit right around the world. The Church is growing daily. The numbers game is perhaps a dangerous one to play here and statistics are never above criticism as they always require interpretation, but perhaps 100,000 (conservative estimate) to 200,000 people (optimistic estimate) are being converted and added to the Church each day around the world. If you keep any kind of watch on the Church internationally, one of the most exciting factors is the way you keep hearing of some new group of churches, another massive individual church, or some new breakthrough of God that you've never heard of before. For example, how many Christians even in England realise that every year in France there is a Bible Week organised by Pentecostal Gypsies that draws together about 45,000 believers? The event is even favourably reported in the French Press.

Returning to Romans, we read an Old Testament quotation, 'Their voice has gone out into all the earth, their words to the ends of the world' (Rom 10:18). In chapter 10, Paul is talking about the preaching of the gospel, and to use this verse indicating the worldwide preaching of the gospel seems exaggeration indeed. But it is surely prophetic. In his spirit, the Apostle could see it. Indeed the fulfilment of it is now at least in sight: the ends of the earth, or every people group, are going to hear the gospel.

In Revelation 5:9 we read, 'And they sang a new song: "You are worthy to take the scroll and open its seals, because you were slain and with your blood you purchased men for God from every tribe and language and people and nation. . . ."' This needs to be taken very seriously as the ground of our confidence for reaching out to every people group. Success is assured because the blood of Christ has been shed. Christ's blood is enough to ensure a harvest among all the peoples of the world.

We need to make practical suggestions as to how to fulfil the big vision and see the gospel of the Kingdom proclaimed to every people group. I find it helpful to speak in terms of Dreams, Teams and Means.

Dreams

We need to dream of people groups and possibilities. Every local church can pray that God will bring to their attention a particular unreached people group. There may be prophecies given that may lead a church in a particular direction, say towards the world of Islam, or to the continent of Africa or South America. In the family of churches to which I belong we once had a prophecy about a bow being drawn back as a prelude to an arrow launch into Europe. Whereas our churches were once almost exclusively in the South East of England, we are now working with and planting new churches in the Midlands and the North. We are drawing back the bow. So we find ourselves preparing and praying for opportunities to plant churches in the many unevangelised parts of the continent as we gather resources behind us. A prophetic word has helped us to dream of possibilities in Europe.

We can take a world map and pray over it and see if God begins to direct us towards a particular part of the world. It is possible to get information about unreached people groups from bodies like the British and Foreign Bible Society. Is God giving us a burden for an area? Is he giving us a dream? We could contribute resources for the work of evangelism and church planting into an unreached group, helping to complete the task that must be done before the Lord returns.

India is surely a key nation here. Estimates are given of some 400 to 500 people groups within its national borders, and the nation's population is set to overtake that of China within the next twenty years.

Teams

We know that Jesus sent out his disciples in twos; there was always the team feel. Jesus himself travelled in a team of men and women. Paul is constantly spoken of as the great church planting pioneer of the early Church, but he was always travelling in the company of other believers. The Apostle worked within a team. If we are going to reach the unreached, we cannot do it in isolation. Single soldiers are easy targets for the enemy – there needs to be a team. Of course history has thrown up the exceptions: extraordinarily gifted, resolute people who have pioneered alone. But exceptions are not good models. The chances are high that we are not one of the exceptions; we need the help and complementary gifting of others if the time comes for us to be personally involved in going.

With teams we need training, which because of so much confusion on this issue today I would want to define separately from discipleship. Discipleship should be, must be, the norm for every believer. 'Jesus said, "If you hold to my teaching, you really are my disciples"' (John 8:31). Discipleship is about hearing and obeying the teaching of Jesus. There are various methods that can be used for 'discipling', but it is essential that people are taught and then in some way held accountable for obedience to that teaching.

To be trained, however, has to do with learning a skill. To plant a church in a new area will be helped by some training. We can't simply rush into cross-cultural evangelism unprepared. There are challenges of language and culture that have to be addressed.

If a church has begun to dream of a particular place to preach the gospel of the Kingdom, it must determine a *strategy* for training people to go to that very place. The dream must be followed by a team.

Means

If the unreached peoples of the world are going to hear the gospel of the Kingdom then the Church must provide the financial means to back it. It is astonishing what huge sums of money can be raised for church buildings at home; it should therefore be possible to raise huge sums of money to reach the nations. Surely a church should not be able to exist comfortably with large sums of money in the bank, but should rather live on the edge of over-spending as money is released to mission. It is a false idea that big churches have a lot of money. Typically, big churches are taking risks, venturing into new areas that will always leave them financially stretched.

The proposition here is not that money should be released to pay national workers or to buy church buildings overseas. As soon as a church is formed in any country it must be encouraged to be self-financing so that it lives trusting God, not a foreign missions board or an overseas church. But where workers are sent to new churches, there must be the means to adequately support their pioneering ministry. The support needs to be in place to enable teams to travel and return frequently to their home church base for refreshing, ministry and prayer. The resources need to be in place to enable supporting and complementary ministry to visit church planters in their pioneering work. Pioneer work can founder because of a lack of financial support and care along with feelings of isolation.

Jesus is going to come again when every people group has heard the gospel of the Kingdom. The Book of Revelation makes it clear that God will call out his nation from every nation, his people from every people, and his tribe from every tribe. If we believe, for example, that Jewish converts will complete such a mission *after* the Rapture and during the Tribulation, then our vision to reach the nations may be lost. But if Jesus is coming back when every people group has been reached then the time for church planting is now.

We must replace any tendency to smallness, which will always be present when churches are concerned largely with their own maintenance, with the big vision of the nations. Whatever size a local church may be, and however small in numbers, it can be big in vision. Every people group must be reached before Jesus comes again. Every local church can really make a contribution to that. We need to surrender small ambitions to a big vision.

Missionary societies and the local church

Today there is much new thinking on the relationship between the missionary societies and local churches. It is important that such thinking neither gives the impression that history is of no importance, nor that the new, radical ideas are short on content and are passing fads. Many missionary societies have made a huge and vital contribution to the evangelisation of the nations. They have also accumulated a vast amount of experience and understanding which, if ignored by those wanting to adopt a more thorough local church approach to mission, could leave them reinventing the wheel in some areas of outreach to the nations. Today there is a genuine shift towards the principle of a local church directly owning its responsibility to world evangelism, with the result that those sent out by them are also the direct and not indirect responsibility of the local church. Missionary societies which remain resistant to this idea may be left behind in the new thing that God is surely doing to reach every people group.

Even the word 'missionary' must be in question today. The Bible uses the terms Apostle, Prophet, Evangelist, Pastor and Teacher. These are the ministries that God raises up to reach the nations of the world. Who is God anointing in our churches today with these gifts, so that – like the early Church – we can lay hands on these people and send them out, fully supported by our local churches to engage in mission to the nations? And, yes, we need all the expertise gained by the older societies to help us in such a task.

The need is immediate. Jesus will return when every people group has received the gospel, which probably means has seen its own church actually established.

We need a big vision for a big work that is still to be done.

Notes

1. Robert Warren, CPAS Review of *Building Missionary Congregations*.
2. Ibid.

13

Unity

Jesus prayed in Gethsemane for the unity of his disciples. Can we seek to be the answer to Christ's prayer in our generation? Again what we believe about the end times can affect our approach to this. Some may believe that such unity can only be reached during the 1000-year reign of Christ on the earth. However if we are not convinced of such an earthly rule then right now is the time to make our contribution to the genuine unity of the Body of Christ.

Unity

Without question the Church comprises all the people of God. Sometimes we hear of the Church militant (that is, the Church on earth) and the Church triumphant (the Church in heaven). What is common to all members of the Church is that they have been redeemed by Christ's blood and born again by the Spirit of God. Denominational labels are irrelevant. The Church comprises all those from every period of history and from every place on earth, whether they have already died or are still living, who have been purchased by Christ's blood and born of his Spirit. The Church will be added to until the full number of Gentiles comes in and all Israel saved before the return of Jesus. At his coming again, the bodies of those who have 'died in Christ' will be raised, the bodies of living Christians will be transformed and Christ's glorified Church and Bride will live and reign with him throughout eternal ages in a restored universe where all things are gathered together again under the Headship of Jesus Christ.

Our present concern is with the living Church on earth comprising all true Christian believers, whether they be gathered in a visible community called a church, or whether for reasons good or bad they belong to no visible church community. Probably in most, and possibly in all such visible communities, there are those not known by God who will be dismissed from his presence on the Day of Judgement.

In the New Testament we see that the Church is viewed as universal and local.

Sometimes the Church is spoken of without any reference to locality – 'Do not cause anyone to stumble, whether Jews, Greeks, or the church of God.' This is a reference to the Church universal to which every Christian belongs. Again we read in Ephesians 5, 'Christ is the head of the church, his body, of which he is the Saviour.' There is no reference to a local church here, but to the universal Church of which Christ is the Head.

The other way in which the Church is spoken of in the New Testament has to do with locality. So we read of the church of God in Corinth or the church of the Thessalonians. The local church is a visible and identifiable part of the universal Church.

We need to note that in the Bible there is nothing between the universal and the local church. There is no national church, such as the Church of England, and there is no denominational church emphasising some particular doctrine, such as the Baptist Church or Pentecostal Church. In Acts 9:31 we do read that the church throughout Judea, Galilee and Samaria enjoyed a time of peace. This is clearly a reference to the churches in Judea, Galilee and Samaria, wherever they were to be found. It would be special pleading to claim that we could view this as the

Church of Judea or the Church of Galilee or the Church of Samaria as though somehow there was reference here to regional churches that were neither local in a city or town nor yet universal.

All the evidence from the New Testament makes it clear that the local church comprised every believer in any given town or city without exception. So when Paul and Barnabas travel up to Jerusalem to debate the issue of circumcision they are greeted by the church in that city, not by a number of different churches. Indeed later on in the chapter we read the expression 'whole church' with reference to the church in Jerusalem. In Acts 20 Paul sends for the Elders of the church at Ephesus, not for Elders from different churches in the one city. In the New Testament there is never any idea of separated churches in the same city.

In Paul's letters to Corinth we have evidence of division in the church there. But Paul still addresses 'the church of God in Corinth' and appeals for perfect unity expressed in mind and thought. On the one hand this appeal by the Apostle suggests it is possible for a church to look disunited. On the other hand it could suggest a church may look united but the real issue is whether there genuinely is oneness of mind and thought – a big challenge! We cannot be satisfied with a cosmetic unity, where real divisions are somehow disguised; but genuine unity tangibly expressed and definitely seen in submission to the word of God.

We can also see that in the New Testament there were subdivisions of the local church as we read several times of the church in the house. This would seem to be a simple description of where the church was meeting and not some dogmatic statement of how the church must meet.

The church would surely meet in any convenient place and in the time of the early Church believers' houses were simply that. Some might suggest that the church in Ephesus met in the lecture hall of Tyrannus, although it appears more accurate to view this as a public centre used by Paul for evangelistic dialogues rather than the actual meeting place for the church in Ephesus. We know from the account of Eutychus falling out of the window during one of Paul's meetings that a church could meet in and pack a home to capacity.

So in a city such as Rome the church would, for the practical reason of needing to meet, gather in as many houses as was appropriate for the size of the church. The Christians who met in each house would be the church in Rome, but all these 'house churches' together would also be the church in Rome.

In a city where the church was meeting in many different houses (or indeed other buildings) the leaders of those different groups would make a vital contribution to the unity of the church as a whole. Today we are in the situation where not only do we allow the use of different buildings in the same city to emphasise that there are different churches in the one locality but even the buildings themselves are called and labelled churches. There is no Biblical warrant for either to happen.

We need to appreciate that in many towns and cities the church requires a number of different buildings to accommodate it. But the individual address is the only way that the church should be spoken of apart from the name of the town or city. So there was the church in Rome, but you could meet with the church in the home of Priscilla and Aquila and presumably the homes of many other Christians as well.

We need to ask the questions: Why do we look disunited? Are we disunited? The following seem crucial factors in this.

1. There is a proliferation of different names for the separated church groups in the same town or city. It is easy to think that our different buildings cause a problem. But the Church needs a number of buildings in which to meet simply because of the size of the Christian community in most towns in the United Kingdom. However many of these buildings are usually named to emphasise differences and separation.

    It is surely questionable whether any building should ever be named as a church. We have seen that in the New Testament the church as the people of God met in houses. Buildings of whatever shape or size can ever only be a place where the church meets. To label a building as a Methodist church, Baptist church or Christian Fellowship etc. marks us out as different to one another and indeed as even wanting to emphasise our differences from one another.

2. Most churches in a town or city, whatever their name, tend to have their primary relationship with churches outside their town or city, rather than within it. These primary relationships are almost certain to be with the denomination or movement to which the church belongs.

3. A lack of unity between churches in the same town can also be demonstrated by a lack of common discipline among those churches. This can be seen in the way a believer may move his membership from church to church in the same town without any contact

between the leaders of those churches. More seriously, should one church excommunicate a member on clear biblical grounds, who is then accepted without investigation into another church in the same town, then relationships between those churches are liable to be strained.

4. Further disunity occurs where leaders fail to honour one another's ministries. Similarly there is a lack of unity of heart and mind when different churches in the same town fail to pray for one another. Sometimes leaders of different churches have sinful attitudes to one another. This usually occurs when, on the basis of insufficient knowledge, criticism is made of other churches or leaders or suspicions are allowed to continue because rumours are not checked out.

There would seem to be three major reasons to stress the need for unity in the Church.

1. The Church does only exist at two levels according to God's word. There is the universal Church and there is the local church. To hold some intermediate position by a primary allegience to a denomination or a particular group of churches may be motivating and temporarily helpful, but it falls short of the biblical standards of unity.

2. The prayer of Jesus:

    'My prayer is not for them alone. I pray also for those who will believe in me through their message, that all of them may be one, Father, just as you are in me and I am in you. May they also be in us so that the world may believe that you have sent me. I have given them the glory that you gave me, that they may be one as we are one: I

> in them and you in me. May they be brought to complete
> unity to let the world know that you sent me and have
> loved them even as you have loved me.' (John 17:20–23)

Commentators will speak of the mystical or spiritual
union that exists between Father and Son because of
their perfect oneness. So we also hear of the mystical
union of the body of Christ. The expression seems to
imply that the Church is one, but don't expect it to
look like that! Jesus' prayer would appear to be for
unity in the Church that is obvious and apparent.
When Jesus prays, 'May they be brought to complete
unity . . .' it surely places a responsibility on each
generation of believers to seek to be the answer to
Christ's intercession.

The fear is sometimes expressed that to talk of
unity is bound to bring a compromise of truth. But we
should note that the prayer of Jesus for the oneness of
his people is in the context of praying for a sanctifying
of God's people by the truth, which is the word of
God. A major part of the Church's search for an
expression of full unity must be to understand what
the truth is and then if there is agreement the challenge
of unity can be met. There is no suggestion being made
by this writer that the Church should seek its unity on
any other basis than the truth of God revealed through
the word of God. Indeed if we have a concern for truth
then we must accept the prayer of Jesus, that his people
should be brought to complete unity, is part of the
truth. Our failure to be the answer to Christ's prayer is
in effect a refusal to obey the truth.

We can emphasise the right basis for unity by also
considering that part of Christ's prayer where he

speaks of believers being given the same glory as the
Father has given to the Son. Any meditation upon that
statement will certainly stagger our imagination.
Surely Christ's glory on the earth was seen by his life
in God. That is also the glory of the believer. Through
Christ we have a life in God. God's Spirit dwells in us
and we have eternal life. So we are certainly talking of
the unity of all those, but only those, who have a life
in God and are indwelt by the Spirit of God. Such is
the glory of every believer, and such glory common to
all believers should again give us every reason for a
definite and tangible unity.

So we should be united because of the prayer of
Jesus. We are not talking of a unity of organisation
that compromises the truth. We are talking of a unity
of those being sanctified by truth, which is the word of
God, and who definitely enjoy the life of God in
Christ that is surely our glory. Indeed it seems incredible that those who share the same glory as was given
to Christ on earth and who are being sanctified by the
same truth can be anything but united.

3. Without unity we lack maturity:

> It was he who gave some to be apostles, some to be
> prophets, some to be evangelists, and some to be pastors
> and teachers, to prepare God's people for works of
> service, so that the body of Christ may be built up until
> we all reach unity in the faith and in the knowledge of the
> Son of God and become mature, attaining to the whole
> measure of the fulness of Christ. (Eph 4:11–13)

These verses clearly suggest that a lack of unity in the
faith indicates immaturity among the people of God.
We are aware of children who quarrel, fall out with

each other and say, 'I won't play with you any more.' It denotes immaturity; something to be expected among young children. However the same attitude can commonly prevail between churches: 'We won't play with you' (or maybe we won't pray with you). This again indicates immaturity. Churches that believe the same gospel and are committed to the Bible as God's word must be showing immaturity if they allow their differences to separate them, rather than their much more important agreement to unite them.

It would be relevant here to comment on the fact that already in Ephesians 4 verse 5 there has been a reference to 'one faith' that is included in a list of those elements constituting our basis for unity. The exhortation at the beginning of Ephesians chapter 4 is to maintain the unity of the Spirit because, among other common elements, we share one faith.

If we take a commonly accepted exposition that this is a reference to justification by faith without which we are unsaved, but is true of all who are saved, then this later reference in Ephesians 4 verse 13 to reaching unity in the faith must refer to the details of the Christian faith about which at present there are disagreements. These disagreements add to (though they do not explain) our disunity. Such differences about the faith might range from the issue of women wearing head coverings in worship to the matter of whether Christ will reign with his Church on earth for 1000 years. Neither these two issues, nor a multitude besides, necessarily have any bearing on whether we are justified by faith, but they can constitute differences about the faith that serve the cause of disunity. Albert Barnes makes this comment on

Ephesians 4:13 about reaching unity in the faith: 'The meaning is, 'til we all hold the same truths and have the same confidence in the Son of God.'[1]

It would seem therefore that a process is necessary. If we are lacking maturity until we all reach unity in the faith we should commit ourselves to work through the differences in the faith that would cause us to separate from one another in the same town or city. In the end there is only one truth; the Bible doesn't leave us with options on issues of doctrine, several of which may be true. If there is one truth on every issue of the Christian faith then we should be in the process of discovering it, and it certainly won't be done by denouncing other true believers or by separating from them. That will only demonstrate immaturity. A unity in the faith will bring us to maturity as the Body of Christ.

It is not uncommon for some to make an appeal to the advantages of diversity as a justification for the many separated churches in the same town. Indeed there are those that suggest this diversity reflects Paul's teaching on the Church as the Body of Christ. So different local churches serve as different members of the One Body. It sounds a reasonable argument, but is actually special pleading to justify an existing situation. It does not really represent the true meaning of Paul's teaching about the Church as the Body of Christ. Paul's argument is that in the One Body each individual believer (not whole congregations!) is a member of that Body with a definite place, and is gifted by the Holy Spirit to make a definite contribution. Paul is illustrating his point from the human body with its different functioning parts, yet together making up one united body. To argue that different churches with a different emphasis are members of the One Body can sound attractive, but it is not what Paul meant.

We need also to be careful that clever 'catch phrases' are not used to justify an unbiblical situation. Some have used the expression, 'We can disagree with one another as long as we are not disagreeable.' Again, this can sound good, but it is not a biblical statement. 'Make every effort to keep the unity of the Spirit through the bond of peace!' and several other similar appeals are biblical exhortations however.

We have behind us a history of separation and division. Gene Edwards, in his book *Our Mission*, writes 'Based on my highly unscientific findings I would venture to say that a Christian worker can expect to pass through a minimum of three major – catastrophic – splits by the time he reaches fifty. So will the typical Christian.'[2] That may reflect the American church scene that is the background to Gene Edwards' writing, but there are plenty of fifty-year-old Christians in the UK who will have a similar testimony! The tendency toward division is not likely to be reversed overnight, but as every journey begins with a first step there needs to be a willingness to move forward step by step toward a tangible and definite expression of unity.

Towards unity

What can we do to demonstrate a greater unity of the Body of Christ in each town or city?

A common leadership

Probably most church members will follow their leaders into either unity or division. It is the leaders who oversee churches that can contribute most to the unity or the separation of the local church. The following points seem vital if leaders are going to build and maintain the unity of the local church.

1. Leaders respecting and honouring one another. They must speak well of one another and not against one another. In situations where doubts and questions are raised about a leader or his church then that leader needs to be spoken to directly by other leaders rather than spoken about.
2. Leaders meeting to pray on a regular basis: for one another, for their congregations, and for the town or city in which they serve.
3. Leaders planning what they can do together. This can include evangelistic outreach, celebrations, agreed statements to the Press on ethical issues, support of social and compassionate ministries such as alternative counselling on the issue of abortion and so on.
4. Leaders exercising discipline together. This will minimise the risk of disorderly or immoral members running from one church to the other without check.

For such a common leadership to work effectively it would probably require the bold step of accepting a leader among leaders in the town or city, just as within any congregation there will usually be such a senior leader. Such a position could be rotated but is certain to work best if the leader with the 'charisma' for such a position is allowed to take it.

The issue of translocal, or what is sometimes called Ephesians 4 ministry, also needs to be grasped. In practice, a form of such ministry is already widely recognised among denominations and movements, although different titles such as Bishop, General Superintendent and Apostle are used. In Ephesians 4 we read: 'It was he who gave some to be apostles, some to be prophets, some to be evangelists, and some to be pastors and teachers, to prepare God's people for works of service, so that the body of Christ may be built up until we all reach unity in the faith. . . .'

Here is the recognition that a wide spectrum of ministry is given to the Church for the building up of the Body of Christ with the aim of promoting unity in the faith – which, as we have seen, leads to maturity. There may be many ministries that can come into a town or city and help that process and should be welcomed. However, we see in the New Testament that although the Apostle Paul would write to and indeed visit the church in Rome (as a prisoner), undoubtedly influencing that church greatly, he was not uniquely their Apostle. To the church at Corinth, however, Paul could refer to a unique relationship. He says: 'Even though I may not be an apostle to others, surely I am to you. . . .' And again, '. . . for in Christ Jesus I became your father through the gospel.' These statements were of course made to a church where Paul had to bring correction in order to assist the church to remain united.

Realistically the Body of Christ in a town or city will need one ministry above others from which it can find input, teaching and wisdom to help bring the church to unity and to maintain that unity. There can too easily be an attitude that is quite distrustful of 'outside' ministry. However, the ascended Christ has given gifts of Apostles, Prophets, Evangelists and Pastor-Teachers to help bring the Body of Christ to unity of the faith.

A common title

This would help to mark out the local church as one church in the eyes both of the members and of those outside the church – if, as suggested earlier, the buildings we use to meet in were only marked by their individual address. What could be helpfully dropped from a title is any reference to denomination and therefore to separation. What is then more obvious for all to see is that there is only one church in any town or city, meeting in different buildings because of size and convenience.

An agreement or covenant

This would require the voluntary commitment and co-operation of all those who presently lead separated churches in the same town. The covenant would declare that the local relationships of the Body of Christ are the primary relationships rather than keeping or promoting denominational (or similar) relationships as those that are primary. It goes without saying that good relationships should be maintained with churches in other towns and cities, and again this would reflect the spirit of the New Testament Church.

Challenges to unity

Firstly, primary relationships of leaders and churches are very often neither universal nor local; they tend to be within a denomination, movement or group of churches. Unless this point is acknowledged, the unity of the local Body will be hindered. No man can be a slave to two masters and neither can a local church! Does the final authority rest within the church in the city or is it ultimately governed by allegiance to wider church group-ings?

Secondly, there are differences about the authority and interpretation of Scripture. There has to be an agreement on the authority of the Bible so it will become possible to maintain unity. Beyond that however there can be differences on how to understand or interpret Scripture on certain issues. The issues may vary from time to time in the history of the Church. Some of the current ones about which opinion is divided could be listed as:

Water baptism
The Holy Spirit
Sovereignty of God/Free will of man
Role of women
Israel

These matters can often tend to assume greater impor-tance in the minds of leaders than of church members. So a believer may belong to a church where the teaching is clearly 'once saved, always saved', and then this member moves to another church where the possibility of losing salvation is taught. Yet the member feels happy in this new church environment irrespective of the doctrinal issues involved.

Nevertheless, issues of biblical interpretation are real issues. Ephesians 4:3–6 suggests that to maintain our unity we need to agree as truth that there is:

One Body	The fellowship of believers
One Spirit	The Holy Spirit who calls all believers to faith
One Hope	The glorious future

One Lord   Christ, to whom we all belong
One Faith   Through which we are justified in Christ
One Baptism   All believers are placed into Christ

One God and Father of us all

If we are agreed on these matters we should work hard not
to let other issues divide us. We have seen that Ephesians
4:13 says, 'until we all reach unity in the faith.' Until we
do we should be prepared to debate our differences either
to a point of common agreement or to the point of
accepted difference but which we refuse to let divide us.

Thirdly, there is the important matter of preference.
There are different styles of church life that touch more
directly on issues of preference rather than strict biblical
interpretation. Some people like drums in a meeting and
some don't! Some like to dance and others don't. Some
want liturgy and others prefer spontaneity. Some leaders
wear church robes, some lounge suits and some T-shirts
and jeans. None of these are matters of direct biblical
interpretation, although there may be some root in
Scripture. They are largely matters of personal preference.
But personal preference can be a divisive issue.

Fourthly, churches and leaders can be very suspicious
of one another. Often this is because a leader or church
members think they know what is happening in another
church fellowship and they disapprove. Sometimes the
suspicion of what is happening can be a lot more exciting
than what actually is happening! But there can be enough
rumours and suspicions to keep churches separated. Such
suspicion is often based on ignorance rather than fact. It
is surely tragic if suspicion and ignorance are allowed to
maintain division.

The other major challenge to unity is the attitude that 'it won't work'. After all, we already have a multiplicity of denominations and movements and they seem to increase all the time, so what hope is there that the situation could be reversed? At one level the growth of new church movements could be seen as very encouraging for it probably demonstrates a growing commitment to world evangelisation. But in our town or city simply to give up on the possibility of the prayer of Jesus being answered seems an unworthy response. In fact it could be argued that in general the People of God today have a greater passion for the unity of the Church than ever before. In Latin America it has already been demonstrated that Christian leaders and churches can come together with a commitment to the unity of the Church and are seeing revival then take place in their communities.

Some suggest that the unity of the Church would be plainly unworkable in a large city like London. But what we see in the New Testament is a church being referred to according to an accepted man-made boundary, e.g. the church in Corinth. Obviously there would be practical difficulties about the church in London demonstrating a meaningful unity. But this could be broken down to, say, the church in Finchley or the church in Bromley. The Christian approach can never be that something looks so difficult it's not worth trying. Rather, what is the word of God saying to us? Jeremiah, reflecting on God's creation of the heavens and the earth, concluded that nothing was too hard for God. Surely that must include the unity of the Church! The God who can create a universe out of nothing can surely bring together the different parts of his Church.

It would be a sterile exercise to seek for unity as an end

in itself. We must ask, what is the purpose for unity? The Bible itself suggests some very definite results.

The purpose of unity

Firstly, a united Church will be the answer to the prayer of Jesus. Nearly two thousand years ago, in agony of spirit in Gethsemane, Jesus prayed for the complete oneness of his people. Through successive generations of Christian history this has never been achieved. Many great truths have been restored to the Christian Church, so why should there not arise a generation of Christians who will genuinely respond to the Gethsemane prayer of Jesus and seek to be the answer. The outcome of such a response rests with God. What really matters is to seek that perfect oneness for which Jesus prayed.

Secondly, we will see the Body of Christ come to maturity and experience more of the whole measure of the fullness of Christ among us. Without our coming to unity of the faith Paul clearly implies that we will miss out on some measure of the fullness of Christ in his Church. There is something experiential here that we do not yet know of Christ's living and moving in his Church, because we remain separated and disunited.

Thirdly, we will enjoy greater evangelistic effectiveness. In John 17:23, Jesus prays: '. . . may they be brought to complete unity to let the world know that you sent me and have loved them even as you have loved me.' Surely the implication here is that our separateness blunts our witness to the world concerning our testimony of Jesus. It is difficult to talk of Christ's love for us when through our disunity we don't look as though we love one another! To talk of Christ's saving power against a background of separation and division does not help us convey the message convincingly. For the Church to be more effective in evangelism the people of God in a town or city must be seen and heard as one.

Finally, we will experience greater blessing in the Church. 'How good and pleasant it is when brothers live together in unity . . . for there the Lord bestows his blessing. . . .' This is a familiar statement, perhaps too familiar. We can use it as a slogan rather than believing in faith that it is true. In many towns and cities of the United Kingdom today there is little blessing. This is not to despise the blessing there is but to acknowledge that it is limited, and to believe that more is surely possible. According to the Bible, blessing is assured – indeed commanded – when God's people live together in unity. When we experience division in our individual congregations we know it brings pain and limits blessing. If in a town or city the church came together as one united body what blessing there must be for the people of God.

In Acts 4:32 we read: 'All the believers were one in heart and mind.' Again it is good to remind ourselves of Paul's words to the church at Corinth, 'I appeal to you brothers in the name of our Lord Jesus Christ, that all of you agree with one another so that there may be no division among you and that you may be perfectly united in mind and thought.'

Both these scriptures suggest to us that unity begins with an attitude of mind and heart, not with an external piece of administration such as re-wording every church notice board to read the same way. Is there a desire in our hearts to reverse the trend of generations and, instead of dividing into more groups, movements and denominations, to look for the unity of the People of God? It is the work of the enemy to divide us, because division causes weakness. Unity brings strength. In the Church of God however there is such a strong pull to doing it 'our way' and with 'our group' of people. If we are going to see the local church expressing real unity it is going to demand change and inconvenience. That's why there needs to be a conviction about this in our mind, together with a heart-felt willingness to commit ourselves in this direction. There are certain to be problems along the way, dis-appointments, checks to our progress, criticism of our motives and misunderstanding of our vision. But will Jesus return for a divided Church or will he return for a Church and Bride that has listened to the passion of his intercession and sought with God's help to become one people in every town or city?

Most of us have known the experience in our Christian life of finding ourselves convinced of something about which we were previously ignorant or resistant to. The Holy Spirit works to bring us revelation and under-standing from the word of God. Could God be speaking to our hearts at this time, impressing upon our minds that the present divided situation of our churches is not right and it is necessary for men and women of courage to take seriously the word of God and the revelation of the Holy Spirit and look for the unity of the Body of Christ? It is not good enough to say that God will do it, as though somehow it will happen apart from us. God will do it through his Church; therefore God will do it through us.

We can only begin where we are, so that in our town or city leaders are seeking out other leaders, showing them respect, building friendships and then praying and working with each other to see the local church as one and so expressing more exactly New Testament church life. It may seem a huge challenge where you live, but nothing is too hard for God!

Over recent years I have made several visits to minister in Cape Town right at the southern tip of South Africa. In past centuries a journey from England to the bottom of the African continent would have taken many months by ship. Earlier this century cruise liners could do the same journey in a matter of weeks. I flew to Cape Town some years ago and the journey took over seventeen hours. On my most recent trip I covered the same distance non-stop in ten and three quarter hours. In other words the journey is getting easier all the time. Years ago to talk of the unity of the Body of Christ might have seemed an almost impossible journey to undertake. But now we can sense that in many places it is getting easier all the time. In many towns and cities there is a greater openness to one another and an increasing desire for the church to come together as one. Prayers for unity are often heard these days.

To see the Church become the answer to Christ's prayer, to become mature, to be increasingly effective in evangelism and to be enjoying God's commanded blessing must surely be motivations for us.

I do not believe that we can wait or even look to some Millennial age in the future, where with Jesus on the earth all the Church is clearly united in a visible way. We surely have a responsibility right now to see the unity of Christ's body; the people for whom he died coming together as one people. Is Jesus going to return for a Church that is demonstrating unity or is visibly divided? Surely we must seek to respond to the heart cry of Jesus in Gethsemane and do what we can to bring together the Body of Christ.

Notes

1. Albert Barnes, *Barnes' Notes on the New Testament*, Kregel Publications, 1980, p. 994.
2. Gene Edwards, *Our Mission*, Christian Books, Auburn, Maine, 1984, p. 1 (Introduction).

14

Now and Then

There is a great deal of speculation about the end of the world. Many today are saying that we are overdue for a massive meteor strike, which would bring to an end life on earth as we know it. Certainly the Bible declares that the end will come but it will be the direct result of the return of Christ. The last enemy to be destroyed is death, but finally, at his coming, Jesus will pick that one off as well. But we need to be concerned for the now as well as the then, when Jesus will return. Everything will be placed under the feet of man, which means right now the Body of Christ is at work in the world extending the reign of Christ, building the local church and engaging in world mission. We anticipate the end and a new beginning.

Now and Then

World history is moving towards a climax, a conclusion and a consummation. As Paul writes in 1 Cor 15:24, 'Then (finally) the end will come'.

There is currently no lack of speculation about the end of the world. The question has been asked as to whether it will happen with a bang or a whimper. Since an A-bomb was dropped on Hiroshima in 1945 most people have inclined to the probability of the bang. The problems associated with over-population are believed by some to be the route to our final destruction. Others point to the fact the sun will eventually burn out to bring an end to life on earth, or maybe we will be the victims of a massive meteor strike.

The Bible not only teaches the end of the world and of history as we know it, but that the end will be inextricably linked to the Return of Christ. 'For as in Adam all die, so in Christ all will be made alive. But each in his own turn: Christ, the firstfruits; then, when he comes, those who belong to him. Then the end will come . . .' (1 Cor 15:22–24).

That the end will come is certain. Either my life will end, or Jesus Christ will come again; I cannot escape the 'then'.

We are living at a time when fewer evangelical churches seem prepared to regularly teach on the Second Coming. This may be because preachers are aware of the many disputes over details of that event. Even the terminology can be daunting; pre-millennial and post-tribulation are not phrases that easily trip off our lips!

In the Bible we find some wonderfully simple statements. 'When he comes' (1 Cor 15:23), 'Then the end will come' (1 Cor 15:24).

It can be exhilarating to try and imagine the return of Christ, for the New Testament gives us enough material to paint a picture. The whole universe will be on the shake preceding the return of Jesus. The Christ whose glory will fill the universe always disturbs the creation. When Jesus was born a star appeared in the sky; when he died darkness fell across the earth; and when he returns stars will fall and planets will shake. A fanfare will announce his arrival. The world will hear the trumpet call of God and the Archangel will shout to announce his coming. I imagine his appearance in the sky will produce joy (if a little nervousness?) on the faces of believers and alarm on the part of those who have not believed. Paul, writing to the Thessalonians, speaks of the splendour of his appearance, and John, as he writes the Revelation, describes the returning Christ as seated on a great white horse. His eyes are a blaze of fire, his robe is dipped in blood, and accompanied by the armies of heaven he will return King of Kings and Lord of Lords.

Then remarkable events begin on the earth as the tombs open up and the bodies of believers are caught up to meet

Christ in the air, instantly transformed as they go. Those still alive on the earth as believers then follow and are transformed into the likeness of Christ as they see him returning in the skies.

These things are definitely going to happen. Then – finally – the end will come and Paul adds that at that time he will hand over the kingdom to God the Father, having destroyed all dominion, authority and power (1 Cor 15:24). We will return to the handing over of the kingdom but here we note that all powers and authorities opposed to Jesus will finally be rendered ineffective. We must never give room to the idea that evil will finally triumph. The end will come and all opposition to Jesus will fall.

We can emphasise this by referring again to the person of the Antichrist. Unfortunately this figure – with his number 666 – does give rise to some fairly wild speculations. We can remove some of the sensationalism by realising that 1 John teaches that the spirit of Antichrist, characterised by opposition to Christ and self-exaltation, has always been at work in the world. Such a spirit has certainly been present in dictators like Hitler, Stalin and Mao Tse-Tung. Such men have cast themselves in the role of their nation's saviour and, while demanding uncritical loyalty and a fanatical commitment akin to religious worship, have begun to execute a reign of terror.

This spirit of antichrist will find its summation in a Man of Evil. At first sight he may look like a world saviour – with the ability to sort out chaos, anarchy and economic collapse. He will seize both political and religious power, demanding worship and total commitment while he pours out his fury on anything that is even suggestive of opposition. So the final days of church history will be marked by great victory amidst a great persecution. Among every people group will be found those who have accepted the gospel, the full number of the Gentiles will come in and all Israel will be saved. But all this will happen as the greatest anti-Christian persecution the world has ever seen takes place. It is reassuring to read the words of the Apostle: 'And then the lawless one will be revealed, whom the Lord Jesus will overthrow with the breath of his mouth and destroy by the splendour of his coming' (2 Thess 2:8). For, then, the end will come and even the man of evil will be swept away.

Sometimes we can feel overwhelmed by the evil in the world. We can wonder, will it get the upper hand and swamp us all? No! Christ will destroy every authority, power and dominion that opposes him. None will stand, all will be rendered ineffective. It's in the Book! It is absolutely certain that we are heading towards a climax and although I do not accept a doctrine of the Church which is triumphalistic, meaning that from here on the Church simply goes from glory to glory with hardly a problem, I do embrace an eschatology which gives me confidence in the final triumph of the Church. When Jesus comes again, the end will come.

It's good to look at the end and what happens then, because it gives us reassurance for the now.

Paul tells us what is happening now in 1 Corinthians 15:25 'For he must reign until he has put all his enemies under his feet.' This cannot mean that Christ will stop reigning when his enemies are destroyed, but Paul is emphasising the present reign of Christ. In the very next verse we read that the last enemy to be destroyed is death. Clearly, that enemy is not destroyed yet, so in the present there are other enemies to be routed. They will be, because there is a Christ who reigns now. It is insufficient to suggest that Jesus will reign as Lord when he returns. He is reigning as Lord now, a fact that will simply be recognised by all when he does return. Neither, as we have seen in this book, can we be satisfied with deferring the reign of Christ to some distant millennium upon the earth. Christ reigns now. He must reign until all his enemies are destroyed and then he will pick off the last one, which is death.

Under his feet

In connection with this we need to pick up the phrase that Paul uses about putting everything under his feet; the most quoted Old Testament phrase found in the New Testament. This is a key scripture for understanding what is happening now. The verse is first found in Psalm 8, where the reference to putting everything under his feet clearly means under the feet of man. This is recognised by the writer to the Hebrews when, having quoted from this passage, he makes the observation 'Yet at the present time we do not see everything subject to him.' This is only honest! But he further adds, 'But we do see Jesus, who was made a little lower than the angels . . .' (Hebrews 2:8–9). So he speaks of seeing Jesus, who was also made man. To understand how everything is placed under the feet of man we need somehow to see it fulfilled in Jesus who himself was made man.

Another use of this quotation comes at the end of Ephesians chapter 1: 'And God placed all things under his feet and appointed him to be head over everything for the church which is his body, the fullness of him who fills everything in every way' (v. 22,23). Here the reference is unmistakably to everything being under the feet of Christ, who is head of his body, the Church. Again in 1 Corinthians chapter 15 the reference is clearly to everything being under the feet of Jesus Christ. How are we to understand this? By comparing the references we can appreciate that Christ invades the Church with grace and power. Everything is placed under our feet when it is placed under his feet. Because Christ reigns and he is the head of the Church, the Church is his agent to bring in his rule and government. More than that, the Church is Christ's body to exercise his reign and rule on earth. As we preach the gospel, as we reach out with compassion to the needy, as we see people healed in response to prayer, as we pull down strongholds of evil and as we build the local church – which is when spiritual warfare is always at its most intense – then we, the Church, demonstrate the reign of Christ.

Certainly the end will come, but what of now? We cannot passively sit on the sidelines waiting for the final whistle (or the last trumpet!). The Church is what Christ is using to express his reign. He will not leave us; he will use us to bring every enemy into subjection and by so doing to bring everything under his feet and ours. Jesus must reign and that is what he is doing right now.

The completeness of Christ's triumph is that there will be a death of death. 'The last enemy to be destroyed is death' (1 Cor 15:26). This needs emphasis for death is the one enemy that finally catches up with everyone. In this life there are many people who escape much in the way of illness, pressure or poverty. Finally, though, death grips us all. We may look young to old age and act young to old age but death will catch up with us. We may dye it, replant it, implant it, lift it or replace it to fight off the ravages of time, but death will get us in the end. When we consider what happens beyond death we are entirely in the realm of

faith; it is the last enemy. But even death will be destroyed
when he comes. The death of death means not only that
no one will die, but also that the dead in Christ will live.
We have already discussed the biblical evidence that tells
us that at death the believer's spirit is released into
Paradise, even then looking forward to the time when
Jesus will come again. The last enemy will surrender to
Christ and even our bodies will live again, though utterly
transformed, for he puts everything under his feet.

In this chapter we have made several references to some
verses in 1 Corinthians chapter 15, but the most mysterious seems to be verse 28. Referring to the time when
everything is under his feet Paul concludes, 'when he has
done this, then the Son himself will be made subject to
him who has put everything under him, so that God may
be all in all.' This raises an important question. In view of
our belief in the Trinity, how can the Son be made subject
to the Father, when they are meant to be forever equal?
The previous verse may serve as a helpful introduction,
'Now when it says that everything has been put under
him, it is clear that this does not include God himself, who
put everything under Christ' (1 Cor 15:27). It is as though
Paul is facing an objection to his teaching when someone
responds to him by saying, 'Well, if everything is placed
under the feet of Christ then that must include God
himself.' Paul answers back by saying, 'It is clear that it
does not include God himself,' almost as though Paul is
saying, 'Don't be silly!'

So in 1 Corinthians 15:28 when the Apostle talks of
Jesus being made subject to the Father there are those who
could respond by saying, 'Well then, this disproves the
doctrine of the Trinity. If there is one God in three
persons, Father, Son and Holy Spirit, but the Son is made

subject to the Father, then the Trinity becomes unequal.' We have to respond by saying, 'Don't be silly! It is clear that it cannot mean that!'

Theologians in their discussion of the Trinity speak of the Trinity as being economic. They mean that the members of the Trinity act in an economic or efficient way to achieve the work of salvation. Jesus willingly submitted himself to his Father's will to come to earth in human flesh and die for our sins. Even now the Holy Spirit is submitting to the will of the Father and Son as he comes to indwell the lives of believers on earth. But in this willing submission there is no loss of eternal equality.

We must therefore see this verse as a reference to the manward and economic function of Christ in completing the work of salvation, and not as a reference to his eternal equality within the Godhead. We speak of the finished work of Christ and that is correct in terms of Jesus having done everything necessary to procure our eternal salvation. But the work of Christ is unfinished in the sense that all that issues from the Cross has not yet been completed. It will be – when he comes. Earlier on in 1 Corinthians chapter 15 Paul speaks of Christ handing over the kingdom to the Father. There is a train of events set in motion by the death and resurrection of Christ, which will only be completed at the return of Christ. Every enemy will be destroyed. Even death itself will be destroyed and Christians raised with new bodies. There will be a restored, reconciled universe; the new heavens and new earth. All this will happen when Jesus comes to complete what his death and resurrection began. It will then be as though Christ turns to the Father and tells him the work is complete. All that he was sent to do as Man has been finished, including the bringing in of a new government.

So the new heavens and new earth will fill with the glory and righteousness of God so that the only description Paul can give is that God will be all in all.

The end will come and the Bible makes it clear that looking at the 'then' – when he comes – ought to be a spur to believers. 'Everyone who has this hope (i.e. of his coming again) in him purifies himself, just as he is pure' (1 John 3:3). So holiness and the Second Coming are inextricably linked. We see this again in Peter's writings, 'But the day of the Lord will come like a thief. The heavens will disappear with a roar; the elements will be destroyed by fire, and the earth and everything in it will be laid bare. Since everything will be destroyed in this way, what kind of people ought you to be? You ought to live holy and godly lives as you look forward to the day of God and speed its coming . . . (2 Peter 3:10–12). How can our holiness speed the day of Christ's return? It is an awesome challenge! Maybe as we live holy lives God is able to invest greater power into his Church and the result of such power could be a renewal or even revival that must always lead to mission. As the mission of the Church takes the gospel to every people group, then the end will come (Matt 24:14). So right now Christ is reigning and the Church has a destiny to fulfil a great prophetic mission on the earth. It is vital that we play our part, living holy lives that can even lead to a speeding up of Christ's return.

We are heading somewhere; the world and certainly the Church are not simply going to peter out. Jesus is coming back, every enemy will be destroyed, and death itself will die.

Then the end will come – a new heavens and a new earth – a new beginning.

Further Reading

A selection of titles that express a variety of views about Eschatology:

David Pawson, *When Jesus Returns*, Hodder & Stoughton, 1995

G. R. Beasley-Murray, *The Book of Revelation*, Oliphants, Revised Edition, 1978

Michael Wilcock, *The Message of Revelation*, IVP, 1975

G. K. Beale, *The Book of Revelation*, Eerdmans, Paternoster, 1999

Robert G. Clouse (ed.), *The Meaning of the Millennium*, IVP, 1977

Iain Murray, *The Puritan Hope*, Banner of Truth, 1975

William Hendriksen, *The Bible on the Life Hereafter*, Baker, 1959

Anthony A. Hoekema, *The Bible and the Future*, Eerdmans, Paternoster, 1979 & 1994

Adrio König, *The Eclipse of Christ in Eschatology*, Eerdmans, Marshall, Morgan & Scott, 1989

David Lawrence, *Heaven*, Scripture Union, 1995

David Pawson, *The Road to Hell*, Hodder & Stoughton, 1992

Rob Richards, *Has God finished with Israel?* MARC, Monarch Publications, 1994; Word, 2000.

Stephen Travis, *Christ will come again*, Hodder & Stoughton, 1982, 1997

Weldon & Levitt, *Is there Life after Death?* Kingsway, 1978

John Piper, *Let the Nations be Glad*, Leicester: Appollos, 1993